CRITICAL PERSPECTIVES ON
THE NEW
COLD WAR

ANALYZING THE ISSUES

CRITICAL PERSPECTIVES ON
THE NEW
COLD WAR

Edited by Bridey Heing

Enslow Publishing

101 W. 23rd Street
Suite 240
New York, NY 10011
USA

Published in 2019 by Enslow Publishing, LLC
101 W. 23rd Street, Suite 240, New York, NY 10011

Cataloging-in-Publication Data

Names: Heing, Bridey.
Title: Critical perspectives on the new Cold War / Bridey Heing.
Description: New York : Enslow Publishing, 2019. | Series: Analyzing the
Issues | Includes bibliographic references and index.
Identifiers: ISBN 9780766098527 (pbk.) | ISBN 9780766098510 (library
  bound)
Subjects: LCSH: United States—Foreign relations—Russia (Federation)—
Juvenile literature. | Russia (Federation)—Foreign relations—United
States—Juvenile literature.
Classification: LCC E183.8.R9 2019 | DDC 327.73047086—dc23

Printed in the United States of America

To Our Readers: We have done our best to make sure all website addresses
in this book were active and appropriate when we went to press. However,
the author and the publisher have no control over and assume no
liability for the material available on those websites or on any websites
they may link to. Any comments or suggestions can be sent by email to
customerservice@enslow.com.

Excerpts and articles have been reproduced with the permission of the
copyright holders.

Photo Credits: Cover, Mikhail Klimentiev/AFP/Getty Images; cover and
interior pages graphics Thaiview/Shutterstock.com (cover top, pp. 3, 6-7),
gbreezy/Shutterstock.com (magnifying glass), Ghornstern/Shutterstock.com
(interior pages).

CONTENTS

INTRODUCTION

The world of international affairs is governed by alliances and treaties, but also tensions between powerful states. At few points in history has the influence of rival nations played out with more consequences for the world order than during the Cold War, a period of conflict between the United States and the Soviet Union that shaped the post-World War II global order. But while the conflict is generally considered to have ended in 1991 with the fall of the Soviet Union, today tension between Russia and the United States remains high, suggesting that the two states are once again entering a Cold War. At the same time, the rise of China as a world power has created tension between that country and the United States, and some worry that a similar conflict could emerge.

The Cold War began in 1947, following the end of World War II two years earlier. Although allied during World War II, the United States and the Soviet Union became intense rivals, challenging each other for military and cultural supremacy over the course of almost five decades. The Soviet Union was made up of a bloc of nations that adhered to communist economic policy under the leadership of Moscow. The United States came to represent the forces of democracy and capitalism, while the Soviet Union advocated for communist economic policy and repressed their people with violent crackdowns on free speech and political expression. The conflict eventually came to an end in 1991, with the fall of the Berlin Wall. Shortly after, the Soviet Union collapsed and the states that formerly made up the union became independent. Russia, although once only part of the Soviet Union, is widely seen as the inheritor of the Soviet Union's legacy.

Although called the Cold War, the United States and the Soviet Union never directly fought one another. Instead, they fought through proxies, or countries where the two could support or directly engage the allies of both countries. Examples of Cold War proxy conflicts include the Vietnam War and conflicts in South America. During these conflicts, the United States and the Soviet Union supported opposing sides, leading to an indirect conflict between the two powers. The direct rivalry between the two countries more often took the form of competition in military, scientific, and cultural developments. The space race and the arms race are two examples of this, as well as the large number of Soviet versus American sporting events in the latter half of the twentieth century.

The Cold War was one of the defining features of the twentieth century, forcing the world into two spheres of influence and feeding conflict around the world. It also posed significant threats to humanity; both the United States and the Soviet Union were nuclear powers, and the threat of nuclear war hung over the decades-long conflict.

Since 1991, the United States and Russia have been tentative allies, working together on some issues but often at odds. This tension plays out more often at the United Nations, where both states have permanent seats on the Security Council, the most powerful body in the institution. The two countries often vote against one another, vetoing global actions or stalling efforts to resolve humanitarian crises. But most often the two countries are able to work together in some capacity, even when heads of the respective states do not get along.

That seemed to change in the early 2000s, however, with the rise to power of Vladimir Putin. Putin has worked to consolidate power in Russia, and at the same time expand Russian influence in neighboring states and the Middle East. The United States has responded by labeling Russia a potential threat to overseas interests. In 2016, Russia took the unprecedented step of appearing to interfere in US elections through disinformation campaigns on social media and leaks of hacked information to the press. The US intelligence community is in agreement that the efforts were intentional and directed by the highest officials in the Russian government.

But as tensions rise again between the United States and Russia, China has also been active in gaining influence around the world. During the Cold War, China was in the midst of an extreme cultural and political overhaul that at times left the country reeling from mass loss of life, but in recent decades China has become a cultural and economic hub for world trade. This shows that although the United States and Russia are returning to familiar patterns of tension, they are doing so in a rapidly changing world order, and it is unclear how a similar cold war will play out today.

CHAPTER 1

WHAT THE EXPERTS SAY

Experts and academics have spent decades sorting through the political ramifications and foundations of the Cold War—the ways in which wars fought as proxy conflicts shaped rising states, how to respond to the proliferation of nuclear weapons that came in the wake of the Cold War arms race, and other lingering questions about the political intrigue that made up that period of history. But recently experts have spotted indications that similar tensions are once again rising, and have spoken out about parallels between today and the Cold War of the past. Pointing to tension between the United States and Russia, as well as the United States and China, experts believe the ramifications of a new Cold War could be dire, and that history poses a way forward toward a diplomatic resolution between these states.

"THIRTY YEARS ON AS 'NEW COLD WAR' LOOMS, US AND RUSSIA SHOULD REMEMBER THE REKYJAVIK SUMMIT," BY DAVID REYNOLDS AND KRISTINA SPOHR, FROM *THE CONVERSATION*, OCTOBER 19, 2016

In what looks very like a tit-for-tat downgrading of bilateral relations, Russia and America have traded diplomatic insults in recent weeks over nuclear weapons, geopolitics and economics, prompting speculation about "a new Cold War".

Moscow acted first, announcing on October 3 that it had suspended its agreement with Washington on the disposal of surplus weapons-grade plutonium. Russian president, Vladimir Putin, accused the United States of "creating a threat to strategic stability as a result of unfriendly actions towards Russia". He cited the recent build up of American forces in Eastern Europe, especially the Baltic states.

For its part, the US suspended talks with Russia over the war in Syria, on top of its existing sanctions against Moscow over Russia's 2014 military actions in Ukraine.

How to escape from this standoff? Are there any lessons to be learned from the era of détente and the end of the Cold War in the 1970s and 1980s? In particular, about the role of international statecraft and personal dialogue between leaders?

ICELANDIC FREEZE

October 2016 marks the 30th anniversary of the summit between Ronald Reagan and Mikhail Gorbachev in

Reykjavik, Iceland which had aimed for an agreement on bilateral nuclear arms reductions. At the time the meeting was depicted in the media as a total failure, particularly over Star Wars, the US plan for a sophisticated anti-ballistic missile defence system. "No Deal. Star Wars Sinks the Summit," *Time* magazine trumpeted on its cover with a photo of two drained and dejected men, unable to look each other in the eye.

The last session ended in total deadlock between the two leaders – maybe a fateful missed opportunity. "I don't know when we'll ever have another chance like this," Reagan lamented. "I don't either", replied Gorbachev. They wondered when – or even if – they would meet again.

This familiar, negative narrative was – and is – shortsighted. In reality, both leaders soon came to a more positive view of the summit. Far from being a "failure", Gorbachev judged Reykjavik to be "a step in a complicated dialogue, in a search for solutions". Reagan told the American people: "We are closer than ever before to agreements that could lead to a safer world without nuclear weapons."

Reagan and Gorbachev had both learned how open discussion between those at the top could cut through much of the red tape and political misunderstanding that ties up international relations. At Reykjavik, even though Stars Wars proved a (temporary) stumbling block, both sides agreed that they could and should radically reduce their nuclear arsenals without detriment to national security. And this actually happened, for the first time ever, just a year later when they signed away all their intermediate-range nuclear forces – Soviet SS-20s and US Cruise and Pershing II missiles – in Washington in December 1987.

The treaty testifies to the value of summit meetings that can be part of a process of dialogue that deepens trust on both sides and promotes effective cooperation. Reagan and Gorbachev clicked as human beings at Geneva in 1985, they spoke the unspeakable at Reykjavik in 1986 with talk of a nuclear-free world – and they did the unprecedented in Washington in 1987 by eliminating a whole category of nuclear weapons. All this helped to defuse the Cold War.

IT'S GOOD TO TALK

Today, however, the world seems in turmoil and trust is once again in short supply. We seem to be back to political posturing, megaphone diplomacy and military brinkmanship. Is there is any place for summitry in a situation of near-total alienation? This question was, of course, at the heart of the easing of hostilities in the 1970s, when East and West tried to thaw relations and find ways of living together peacefully.

Helmut Schmidt, West Germany's "global chancellor" of the 1970s, was a great practitioner of what he called "Dialogpolitik". He argued that leaders must always try to put themselves in the other person's shoes in order to understand their perspective on the world, especially at times of tension. He favoured informal summit meetings as a way to exchange views privately and candidly, rather than feeding the insatiable media craving to spill secrets and proclaim achievements.

In the early 1980s, when superpower relations were stuck in a deep freeze, Schmidt conducted shuttle diplomacy as the self-styled "double-interpreter" between Washington and Moscow. Even when no real deals were in the offing, he believed it particularly vital to keep talking.

The German chancellor, Angela Merkel, recently revived Schmidt's approach, emphasising the need to maintain lines of communication with the Kremlin at a time of renewed East-West tension. Equally, however, she has insisted on the importance of a strong defence capability. Merkel is surely right. There is always a delicate balance to be struck between the diplomacy of dialogue and the politics of deterrence – making up your mind when to reach out and when to stand firm. Three decades on from Reykjavik, that remains the perennial challenge for those who have the vision, skill and nerve to venture to the summit.

1. What parallels does the author see between the Cold War and the diplomatic relations between the United States and Russia today?

2. What does the author think politicians can learn from Reykjavik and how can those lessons be applied to tensions today?

"THE REAL WINNER OF THE UKRAINE CRISIS COULD BE CHINA," BY GABRIELA MARIN THORNTON AND ALEXEY ILIN, FROM *THE CONVERSATION*, FEBRUARY 23, 2015

The crisis in Ukraine has plunged US-Russian relations to their lowest point since the Cold War.

Crimea is now Russian territory. Although prisoners of war have been exchanged and both sides have agreed to pull back heavy weapons, the accord signed on February 12 in Minsk has failed so far to stop the fighting in Eastern Ukraine. The city of Debaltseve has fallen into the hands of the separatists. On Sunday a bomb exploded at a rally in Ukraine's second largest city Kharkiv killing two – the suspects are accused by the Ukrainian government as having been trained in Russia.

For Washington, the conflict between the West and Russia has become much more than a conflict over Ukraine's territorial integrity. It has become a provocation to the Western liberal international order that the US worked hard to create at the end of the Cold War; an order based on democracy, the rule of law, and free markets. Russia has not gone down this road. Instead, it is now challenging the European security order and most particularly the Eastern European states.

Talk of a new Cold War has emerged in Washington political circles. Similar views are echoed in Moscow. Konstantin Sonin, a professor at the Higher School of Economics in Moscow, says of the Kremlin's thinking: "The country [Russia] is on a holy mission. It's at war with the United States."

In pushing to impose sanctions against Moscow (and possibly arm the Ukrainians), US policymakers seem to have given little thought to the long-term geopolitical impact of this rift on relations with China.

If there is no viable solution to the Ukrainian conflict, we believe that the unintended "winner" of the crisis could well be China.

Here's why.

CHINA RISING

According the International Monetary Fund, China has now surpassed the United States as the world's number one economy as measured by purchasing power parity. Beijing is also engaged in a major military buildup. Like other emerging great powers in history - especially the US in the late 19th century - China seeks to emerge as the dominant power in its own region.

Russia is helping to fuel China's rise. If the US and Europe don't mend their adversarial relationship with Russia, China will be in a position to counteract the US even sooner.

Russia's economy is tanking because of collapsing oil prices and Western sanctions. The World Bank now projects that Russia's gross domestic product (GDP) will decline by 2.9% in 2015. And the European Bank for Reconstruction and Development estimates that Russia's economy will shrink by close to five per cent this year.

In a desperate attempt to stave off economic disaster, Russia is turning towards Asia to sell its natural resources, obtain loans and forge new military arrangements.

In May 2014, for example, Moscow and Beijing signed a US $400 billion gas deal. In November 2014, another framework agreement for gas supply to China was signed. In September 2014, then-US Defense Secretary Chuck Hagel pointed out that China and Russia are jointly developing new weapons systems. Russia's trade with China is expected to increase to $100 billion this year from $90 billion in 2014.

FAUSTIAN BARGAIN

The two-fold logic of this rapprochement is simple: China needs resources and Russia has them. Russia needs markets, foreign investment, and money and China has them.

Geopolitical interests also overlap. China does not want the South China Sea dominated by Americans. Russia does not want the West – the US and Europe - to penetrate what Moscow perceives as "its sphere of influence." In short, Russia and China do not want a world dominated by the US. That much is clear.

At the same time, China and Russia are geopolitical rivals. Indeed for Russia, its links to China are a Faustian bargain.

In the short term, Russia gains by selling oil, gas, and other natural resources to China. In the longer term, however, the consequence is to further strengthen the emergence of a China that seems fated to be Russia's long-term competitor. Moscow is helping China to grow economically and become more powerful even as Russia itself is becoming weaker.

REALPOLITIK

European leaders are rightly alarmed by the situation in Ukraine. The casualties are mounting and Ukrainian economy is on the verge of collapse. A solution to the crisis needs to be found.

There is a lot of talk, especially in Washington, about the "post-Soviet space" - the former republics of the Soviet Union (like Ukraine) that gained independence following the Soviet collapse. US and European policymakers need to remember that the post-Soviet space was also the pre-Soviet space - the Tsarist Russian empire. Russia still sees itself as the dominant power in a region in which history and culture give it special interests. While the redrawing of Europe's map, as Vice President Biden puts it, is unacceptable, it is a fact on the ground that will be difficult to undo.

Despite understandable condemnations of the Russian moves, negotiations with Moscow should continue.

Longer term, the US needs to think about how to be a triangular great power. Most US strategic thinkers agree that it is China, not Russia, that poses the most significant 21st century geopolitical challenge to the United States. Strategy 101 would then dictate that Russia should be a counterweight to rising China.

But at the moment US (and European) policy is pushing Russia into China's arms. This, we would argue, is a geopolitical mistake. If the US-Russia rift is not healed, it is China that will be the winner.

1. How does China factor into the conflict in Ukraine, according to the author?

2. What is China's relationship to the United States and Russia in the context of a "new Cold War"?

EXCERPT FROM "THE ROLE OF THE 'NEW COLD WAR' CONCEPT IN CONSTRUCTING RUSSIA'S GREAT POWER NARRATIVE," BY IONELA MARIA CIOLAN, FROM *CENTER FOR EUROPEAN STUDIES WORKING PAPERS*, VOLUME VIII, ISSUE 4

The Ukrainian crisis and the annexation of Crimea have opened a new chapter of divergences between the West and Russia. While the United States and the European Union adopted economic sanctions on major Russian state companies, banks and several high level officials for the annexation of Crimean Peninsula (BBC, 2014), Russia responded by banning certain EU agro-food products (McEldowney, 2016). Moreover, in April 2014 NATO suspended all practical cooperation with Russia, including NATO-Russia Council (only three meetings for the past two years, all of them in 2016) (NATO, 2016a).

Numerous events that occurred in the 2014-2016 period deepened further the shaken cooperation between the West and Russia: from Russia' support of the far-right parties in Europe[1], to MH17 Malaysia plane crash in Donbas (above the area controlled by the separatists) with a Russian-made surface-to-air BUK missile (Parket, 2016), to Russia' support for the al-Assad Government and its involvement in the Syrian conflict, to the alleged Russian hack on the American elections and cyber-attacks on American media outlets[2]. In addition, disagreements concerning the implementation of the Minks Agreements and recent tensions between Kiev and Moscow about an alleged "terror" claim conducted by the Ukrainian intelligence services in Crimea[3] complicate furthermore the relations. In the same time, the European Union and the US announced that they will continue with the economic sanctions (European Council, 2016) and NATO will deploy four battalions on Eastern Europe for deterrence purposes (as decided in the Warsaw Summit in July 2016). Those decisions have more reasons for observers' claims that Russia and the West are on the verge of a "New Cold War".

Within this context, more and more Western media, think thanks or various academic voices are speaking about the concept of "New Cold War". Not only Western outlets are using this concept, but what is even more challenging is that also high officials from Russia started to refer to it in public discourse. Most recently, during the 52nd Munich Security Conference in 2016, Russian Prime Minister Dmitry Medvedev declared that "The political line of NATO toward Russia remains unfriendly and closed. It can be said more sharply: We have slid into a time of a new Cold War" (Meyer et al., 2016), warning that the Western countries and the US do not follow any more the Post-World War II security architecture that brought peace and stability to the continent and the only way to avoid it is through cooperation. While Jens Stoltenberg, the Secretary General of the Alliance, in the statement of the NATO Summit in Warsaw, dismissed the allegations of a possible new Cold War by saying that: "*NATO doesn't seek confrontation, we don't want a new Cold War. The Cold War is history, and it should remain history*" (NATO, 2016b).

Nevertheless, there is a shared view expressed by a segment of influential international experts stating that starting with 2014 the relations between the United States and Russia are *"at their lowest point since the end of Cold War"* (Stavridis, 2016). Moreover, as Michael Ignatieff suggests, the Ukrainian crisis highlights the new structure of the post-Cold War order as *"we seem to have the reproblematisation of post-Soviet borders everywhere from the Baltics, through the Balkans, through Poland, through Romania, through Georgia"* (Ignatieff, 2014, p. 4). Beyond various contradictory opinion, one thing is evident that tensions have rose between the US and Russian Federation on frictions concerning the conflict in Eastern Ukraine and the annexation of Crimea, different views regarding possible solutions for the Syrian crisis and the buildup of NATO and its troop exercises near the borders of Russia. And Russia's dissatisfaction, together with its concerns for the security of Kaliningrad are leading to a downgrade to a Cold-War mentality that was translated in practice, in the spring of 2016, in two risky manoeuvres of flyover of Russia's over a U.S. warship in the Baltic Sea and a U.S. aircraft in the international space nearby (Stavridis, 2016).

Keeping in mind the situation briefly described above, this article will analyse the concept of the "New Cold War" and particularly how this concept is used by Russia in the international community to reinforce the country's great power status and the projection of its position/role in the new world order. We are initializing our research with our research question: "How the "New Cold War" concept fosters the idea of the Russian Federation as a great power?". During this paper, we will assess the assumption that the "New Cold War" is a symbolic concept used to strengthen Russia's 'Great Power Narrative' (GPN).

...

1. CONCEPTUALIZING THE "NEW COLD WAR"

The Cold War was a significant historical period that shaped the behaviour of the world for more than half of century. The fundamental characteristic of the Cold War period was its clear bipolarity that divided the world in two camps on the West-East sloap (on one side there was the Western Bloc, led by the United States and on the other the Eastern Bloc with the Soviet Union in charge), which was sustained by a fierce ideological battle (liberalism/capitalism versus communism/socialism). During this period, both parties tried to 'demonize' the enemy and fabricate ominous attributes about the other. Moreover, other important elements include the existence of two military alliances (NATO vs. the Warsaw Pact), two different economic systems, the threat of mutual nuclear annihilation, proxy wars. The appeal to reason, morals, law or the attempt to understand the other's point of view was disregarded in favour of oneself's interests and ideas.

For the past twenty five years, speaking about the end of Cold War was a leitmotif in international relations. But as Michael Cox underlines, using analogies to the past to understand the current events was an overused recurrent exercise even though a legitimate one (Cox, 2014). Therefore, the literature is abundant with articles referring to the "Cold War" and analogies of a new "Cold War". From ideas that associate global terrorism to a new cold war (Buzan, 2006), to analogies to religious nationalism (Juergensmeyer, 1993), or energy security (Kandiyoti, 2015; Ciuta and Klinke, 2008) to US-China relations (Shambaugh, 1995), or the confrontation of political Islam with the Western model (Salla, 1997), and more recently Cyber espionage (Jones, 2016) and cybersecurity (Moss, 2013), these are just few attempts of the past two decades to categorize some international events according to history and integrate them into a familiar framework. The concept of Cold War is *"a contemporary international relations metaphor for a fundamentally strained relationship that cannot be resolved within the framework of the world views of either party but requires a rethinking of both"* (Sakwa, 2008, p. 26).

The frequency of the term "New Cold War" both in academia and mass-media has reached a high level with the Ukraine crisis and the worsening relations of the West with Russia. For Legvold, the annexation of Crimea by Russia is the starting point of the new cold war. In his conception, this war will be different from the original in intensity and ideology. Even if it will have an effect on the international affairs it will be a limited war between Russia and the West. Moreover, some of the patterns that were distinct for the Cold War (ideology driven objectives) are lacking but the political animosity is replacing that gap (Legvold, 2014).

The "New Cold War" concept does not have a commonly acknowledged definition and that is why various experts have different approaches to the term. Some scholars consider that we are already in a new Cold War regardless of the fact that this one does not have the characteristic elements of the classical one (Cohen, 2014). Acknowledging the profound changes that Russia faced since the demise of USSR and its integration into the capitalist system, its actions towards its neighbours, its rising nationalist discourse, its perception as a great power and its anti-West attitude are characteristics common to the Cold War mentality and should not be disregarded (Cox, 2014).

Others like Gromyko consider that a new Cold War is most unlikely since the world in which we live is a poly-centric one. Nevertheless, the author doesn't deny the re-appearance of opposing political and military alliances with a different ideological path, either real or constructed. On this argument, he suggests the idea of a possible "small Cold War" that will be limited in action and impact (Gromyko, 2015).

For Richard Sakwa, a "New Cold War" represents the results of the inability to efficiently prevail over the structures and sentiments that accompanied the "original struggle" (Sakwa, 2008). Nevertheless, since the world is not split anymore between the two rival ideological projects used by the US and Russia, the conditions for a Cold War reappearance following its classical patterns are not present. In his view, bipolarism is not valid any longer as the relations of Russia with the United States do not represent anymore the nucleus for the world politics (Sakwa, 2008).

While some scientists are already admitting the existence of a New Cold War world, others are declining this assumption.

As we can see from the definitions presented above, there is not a unified acceptance of the possibility of a new Cold War, its characteristics or the type of its impact. The common ground found in the literature review is that all authors support the idea that a return to the bipolar system it is improbable as the structural changes held for the past twenty-five years both in Russia and the U.S. and the appearance of other important political and economic players (China, India, Japan, Brazil, the European Union) makes the idea of a clear demarcation between two politically-military blocs impossible. In addition to the elements presented in this section, we want to accentuate that the transformative nature of the globalized system created a dependency between states that cannot easily and without enormous cost can be rearranged.

While we are accepting the fundaments of the "New Cold War" concept (the political animosity between Russia and West, the probability of a small scale conflict, the nuclear threat and the fact that an eventual "new Cold War" will be low in intensity and territorial impact), we depart from the other definitions by stating that we consider this term to have a strong symbolic meaning. The distinction is that we view the "New Cold War" as a tool that can play an ideological purpose if empowered by policy makers.

...

CONCLUSION

The annexation of the Crimean Peninsula and the conflict in Ukraine open a Pandora box in the international community. Questions about the end of the unipolar order and what should we put in place, started to be more present in the academic, think tank and media environments. In this highly volatile and complicated international context we tried throughout this paper to analyse the Russian foreign policy. We started our research from the assumption that the "New Cold War" is a symbolic concept employed by the Russian foreign policy agenda to strengthen its great power status and promote the need for a multipolar world.

After conducting a thoroughly contextualization of the foreign policy agenda of the Russian Federation and its main important events for the past decade, we dealt with the conceptualization of the "New Cold War" term.

The preliminary findings show us that Russia adopted an assertive and pragmatic great power attitude starting with 2007. That was translated into a more confident, bold and risk-taking external relations approach.

Another important result is that Russia tries to obtain international recognition for its status as a great power. In this regard, we can analyse the term of the "New Cold War" suitable for the case. Symbolically, the concept holds the meaning of a shift in the international system.

As such, the possibility of a "New Cold War" can also be perceived as carrying on the beliefs of the former Cold War. Nevertheless, the interesting finding is that Russia is not promoting a return to Bipolarism, but rather the model of multipolarity where the country is an equal international participant as the other actors (states).

Keeping in mind, that the international context that is observed in this research is still unfolding and changes to the West-Russia relations are happening at a higher intensity, the preliminary findings of the author confirm this article main idea: "New Cold War" is a symbolic concept used to strengthen Russia's great power narrative with the objective of deconstructing and constructing a new set of norms and rules that define the institution of the international system.

1. The author of this research paper gives several explanations of the term "the new Cold War." Which do you most agree with and why?

2. This paper argues that the Russian government has encouraged the use of this term and its related narrative for political reasons. What are these reasons?

"CYBER ESPIONAGE AND THE NEW COLD WAR OF US-CHINA RELATIONS," BY TIM STEVENS, FROM *THE CONVERSATION*, MAY 21, 2014

The members of China's military charged over cyber espionage by the US will never see American justice, but the case does break new ground in a fractious US-China relationship increasingly characterised by mutual accusations of foul play. What does this mean for relations between the US and China? Might other countries follow this precedent with their own legal actions?

The US and China have been wrangling over this issue for years. Congressional committees complain about theft of US intellectual property by Chinese firms like Huawei and portray them as proxies of the Chinese government.

Post-Snowden, China has retaliated by drawing attention to leaked documents suggesting the US National Security Agency regularly hacks Chinese networks.

The White House indicates that "cyber issues" are central to Sino-American relations, although this is a relationship so soured that two recent authors describe the effects of "cyber" on bilateral relations as "toxic" and "poisonous".

In February 2013, cyber security company Mandiant traced many alleged Chinese activities to a Shanghai industrial estate and specifically to People's Liberation Army (PLA) Unit 61398 located there.

Mandiant claimed the unit was responsible for commercial cyber espionage against US interests, an accusation Beijing firmly rejected. The Obama administration hoped this "naming and shaming" tactic might force new Chinese President Xi to rein in the PLA or at least get them to be less brazen in their operations.

This message did not reach the PLA. After a brief lull, Unit 61398 was back in operation and five of its officials feature in the new indictments, charged with stealing proprietary information from American companies engaged with state-owned Chinese businesses. The stark accusation is: these individuals are part of a state-led conspiracy to steal intellectual property from American companies with whom China has legitimate business. This material includes internal email exchanges and "trade secrets related to technical specifications for nuclear plant designs".

THE REAL REASON FOR AMERICA'S ANGER

What infuriates the US is not the use of computer networks for secret espionage—after the Edward Snowden spying revelations it can no longer deny the extensive nature of its own national intelligence activities—but what it sees as the subversion of the rules of free enterprise. This spat is about commercial espionage and specifically US enterprise not ceding strategic advantage to Chinese competitors. The US wants a level commercial "playing field" and it perceives Chinese actions as inimical to that.

China has denied the charges as "made-up" and reasserted it does not engage in such activities. The US says it will issue further indictments against individuals suspected of conducting commercial cyber espionage. Given US prosecutors know the chance of prosecuting PLA officials in person is effectively nil, what function do these indictments serve and what happens next to US-China relations?

SENDING A MESSAGE

The indictments may be symbolic because they will not result in prosecutions, but this does not mean they are meaningless. They put pressure on Beijing to be seen doing something constructive, rather than making generic denials of illegal activity. They also signal that China must do so or risk as-yet unspecified consequences. This is perhaps not such an empty threat given the details of the indictments also communicate strongly to the Chinese that US intelligence has good operational knowledge of the PLA's networks and even individual officials.

Will this spark similar legal moves by others? US allies like the UK and Australia have their own complaints about Chinese cyber espionage but they might prefer the US takes the diplomatic flak rather than commence their own rather less muscular legal challenges. Alternatively, the US might pressure them to do just that, to communicate to China that the international community is just as concerned about Chinese actions as they are.

How China responds is critical, not because it is necessarily at fault, but because in the diplomatic game Beijing must react to an escalatory gambit like this. Will it respond in kind, or might it switch to the sort of diplomatic tit-for-tat that characterised the Cold War?

If China decides, for example, to indict Keith Alexander, the former NSA director implicated in cyber operations against China, it will look petty and bereft of ideas. If history is any guide, however, we can expect China to claim the moral high ground while continuing much as before, which will enrage the Americans.

Each side accuses the other of avoiding constructive dialogue but neither has found a way of saving face so that such engagement might take place. This latest move makes it even less likely that the two sides can sit down together and China has already suspended a US-China internet working group, indicating a further chill in bilateral relations. The US and China need this mutual relationship to work but this latest development shows again how hard they both find it to manage. Your move, Mr President.

1. How is China using cyber espionage against the United States?

2. What does the author think this indicates about relations between the two states?

"ARE EUROPE AND THE WORLD SLIPPING BACK INTO A SECOND COLD WAR?," BY FILIP SLAVESKI, FROM *THE CONVERSATION*, NOVEMBER 18, 2014

Bloodshed in Europe and the Middle East against the backdrop of a breakdown in the dialogue between major powers is of enormous concern. The world is on the brink of a new Cold War, some are even saying that it has already begun. – Mikhail Gorbachev

Gorbachev may be right, but the "new Cold War" is very different to the old one. At the end of the Second World War in 1945, many within the Soviet and American governments had a genuine sense that their wartime alliance should continue. They hoped it would form the cornerstone of a peaceful and prosperous post-war world order divided into their respective spheres of influence.

The bankrupt Brits, in the throes of losing their empire, were less enthusiastic. So too were the Soviet and American hardliners whispering in the ears of Stalin and Truman.

By 1947, the goodwill had vanished. The hardliners were screaming as serious conflicts over Germany, Poland and Iran developed. By 1948, the Soviets and the West were in a standoff over Berlin. By the end of the decade, the Cold War had come to Asia, especially Korea, under the threat of mutually assured destruction by nuclear weapons.

TESTING THE LIMITS OF
SPHERES OF INFLUENCE

The question of what went wrong after 1945 to spark the Cold War has long occupied and divided historians. One key problem was that none of the major powers shared the same understanding of where their spheres of influence began and ended.

For all of their protestations, the British and Americans had to accept that Poland fell within the Soviet sphere of influence in Eastern Europe. Yet they drew the line at Stalin's armed support for communist rebels in oil-rich Iran at the beginning of 1946. This was Britain's backyard; Stalin had no place in it.

Though Stalin was testing the boundaries of his sphere of influence and quickly withdrew his troops from Iran, the hardliners interpreted the Soviet Union's behaviour in Iran as part of a growing communist expansionism. They interpreted pretty much everything else the Soviets did thereafter in the same way. This misinterpretation elicited a similar one from Moscow and Cold War was now well under way.

Misinterpretations still abound in relations between Russia and the west, but today these are less about where one's sphere of influence begins or ends. The European Union (EU) clearly no longer considers that Russia or anyone else has a legitimate sphere of influence at all in which they can operate to maintain their strategic interests.

TODAY'S FLASH POINT: UKRAINE

Many in the EU have stopped thinking in these or even geopolitical terms. Theirs is a post-nation-state universe of co-operation among partners for which military conflict is unimaginable.

After years of division and economic disaster, the pro-EU protests in Kiev a year ago reinvigorated this vision among EU idealists and expansionists in Brussels. For them, Ukraine is part of their united Europe and the next logical next step in the European project.

This logic is central to understanding why the EU worked so hard to help oust Viktor Yanukovych and "facilitate" a transition "government" that would accept their fantastic promises of huge money and even long-term integration. Neither promise looks likely to be met.

It explains why so many EU leaders failed to anticipate Russian president Vladimir Putin's response to this "revolution", which overthrew his ally Yanukovych and replaced him with a loose and unstable coalition of largely anti-Russian politicians.

The broader problem is that outside EU elites within Europe, not many other people live in the EU universe. Russia and Ukraine certainly don't live there. This is slowly becoming apparent to many in the EU as frustration grows in Brussels with delays in improving endemic corruption in Ukraine and the financial burden it poses.

At the same time, Russia's involvement in the conflict in eastern Ukraine continues. The exact nature and degree of this involvement is still unclear, as is the matrix of agents involved in this civil war.

Beyond a ramshackle Ukrainian national army and disparate rebel forces under competing commands, there are also mercenary armies under the control of local oligarchs and volunteers from both Russia and Ukraine. Some seem to be operating beyond organised military command structures. Russian special forces may also be involved. Civilians are stuck somewhere in the middle and suffering from all sides.

SEEING PUTIN AS STALIN REBORN

The US tactic of putting pressure on Putin to do this or that in Ukraine and punishing Russia with sanctions when he fails to respond has never recognised this chaotic reality. This is despite many impartial observers on the ground reporting this fact. The Obama administration seems to see Putin as the puppet master in the same way as their predecessors saw Stalin.

The US response is not to recognise Russia's sphere of influence beyond its own borders (not including Crimea), thus not recognising one at all. This is an extreme form of neo-containment policy unimaginable even to Cold War warriors. And it is being pursued (poorly) by an administration that is increasingly seen as incompetent in managing foreign affairs.

If not incompetent, then the Obama administration is at least unwilling to understand how American foreign policy in its self-designated "sphere of influence" in the Middle East over the past decade has taught others how big powers are supposed to behave. Putin is an avid observer.

The "new" Cold War is not as serious a threat to global security and even humanity as the old one. Some of the players aren't even fighting over the same things now as they were in the "old" war. But misinterpretations still abound and these were and remain at the root of both wars. Where they will grow remains to be seen.

1. How does the author describe relations between the Soviet Union and the European Union?

2. Explain spheres of influence and their relationship to the Cold War.

"RUSSIA'S SHADOW-WAR IN A WARY EUROPE," BY SEBASTIAN ROTELLA, FROM *PROPUBLICA*, APRIL 4, 2017

As the French prepare to vote Sunday in a presidential election marked by acrimonious debate about Russian influence in Europe, there's little doubt about which candidate Moscow backs.

Last month, the combative populist Marine Le Pen of the right-wing National Front flew to Moscow to meet with President Vladimir Putin. It was a display of longtime mutual admiration. The frontrunner in a field of 11 candidates, Le Pen shrugs off allegations of corruption and human rights abuses against Putin, calling him a tough and effective leader. Her hard-line views on immigration, Islam and the European Union win praise from Putin and enthusiastic coverage from Russian media outlets. Her campaign has been propelled by a loan of more than $9 million from a Russian bank in 2014, according to Western officials and media reports.

Meanwhile, aides to Emmanuel Macron, the center-left former economy minister who is Le Pen's top rival, have accused Russia of hitting his campaign with cyberattacks and fake news reports about his personal life. Although French officials say the computer disruptions were minor and there is no conclusive proof of links to the Russian state, President François Hollande and other leaders have warned about the risk of interference comparable to hacking operations that targeted the U.S. elections. The French government, aided by briefings from U.S. agencies about their experience last year, has beefed up its cyber defenses.

American politics was jolted when 17 intelligence agencies concluded in January that Russia had covertly intervened in the 2016 presidential campaign with the aim of electing Donald Trump. Such activity is nothing new in Europe, where Russia has launched a series of clandestine and open efforts to sway governments and exert influence, according to European and U.S. national security officials, diplomats, academics and other experts interviewed by ProPublica in recent weeks.

"The Russians have had an aggressive espionage presence here for a long time," a senior French intelligence official said. "The Russians now have more spies, more clandestine operations, in France than they did in the Cold War."

European and U.S. security officials say Russian tactics run the gamut from attempted regime change to sophisticated cyber-espionage. Russia has been linked to a coup attempt in Montenegro (the Balkan nation had dared to consider joining NATO); an old-school spy case involving purloined NATO documents and an accused Portuguese double agent; a viral fake news story about a 13-year-old girl in Germany supposedly raped by Muslims, and a caper by suspected Russian hackers who briefly seized control of an entire television network in France.

"One of the reasons Russia has been so successful has been its ability to develop tactics and techniques it selectively uses depending on the target country," said Andrew Foxall, director of the Russia Studies Center of the Henry Jackson Society, a London think tank. "There's a nuance to it as well. That's something that in the West we fail to grasp."

The French elections are the latest front in what is likely to be a conflict for years to come. Officials say France and Europe are vulnerable because of converging crises: immigration, terrorism, structural economic inequities, the Brexit vote in Britain last year, the rise of populism and extremism. The French election offers a particularly tempting target to the Kremlin, which wants to weaken and divide the West and multinational institutions such as the European Union and NATO, according to Western officials and experts.

Le Pen's proposed policies align closely with Moscow's geopolitical goals. She promises to reinstate national borders, abandon the euro currency and hold a referendum on whether France — which will be the EU's remaining nuclear power after Britain's departure — should remain in the 28-member bloc.

"For Russia, there is a desire to display power," said Thomas Gomart, director of the French Institute of International Relations, a think tank in Paris. "They have openly chosen their candidate. It's very serious. If Le Pen is elected, which is not impossible, that would be part of a chain of events including the Brexit and the election of Trump that would amount to a spectacular reconfiguration of the Western political family. The Russians want to weaken Europe, and to break NATO. The stakes are very high."

Pre-election polling in France shows that no candidate has enough support to receive the required 50 percent, which means the likely result of Sunday's vote will be a May 7 runoff pitting Le Pen against Macron or another strong challenger. Experts worry about a potential Russian spy operation, such as a Wikileaks-style disclosure of compromising information about a candidate, intended to tip the scales during that showdown.

No such direct intervention has been detected to date, and Russian officials reject allegations that they are trying to manipulate elections in France or elsewhere.

The Putin government has "no intention of interfering in electoral processes abroad," said Dmitry Peskov, a Kremlin spokesman, in February. He complained about "a hysterical anti-Putin campaign in certain foreign countries."

Intelligence operations — especially in the high-tech realm — are difficult to pin conclusively on a state. Moreover, Russian spy agencies have developed sophisticated capabilities in the gray areas of information warfare and political influence.

"We don't see cyberattacks for the moment here affecting the campaign," the senior French intelligence official said. "There are Russian influence efforts, news coverage by Russian media, the standard activity. But most of it is not illegal."

Even some Western intelligence officials concerned about Moscow's aggressiveness think there is a tendency to exaggerate the problem. Although European experts generally agree with the U.S. intelligence community's conclusion that Russia interfered with the presidential race last year, those interviewed did not think it had a decisive impact on the victory of President Trump.

"Russia's impact has been greatly underestimated, but it shouldn't be overestimated either," Gomart said.

As far as European spy-catchers are concerned, the Cold War is back — if it ever ended. An early sign came in 2006 with the assassination of Russian exile Alexander Litvinenko in London.

Litvinenko was an outspoken foe of Putin and a veteran of the powerful Federal Security Service (FSB), which Putin once led. In 2000, Litvinenko fled to London. He spent the next few years helping British and Spanish intelligence and law enforcement investigate ties among Russian mafias, politicos and security services.

In November 2006, Litvinenko died after three weeks of agony as the result of being poisoned with polonium-210, a rare radioactive toxin, by two Russian agents at a luxury hotel in London, according to a British court inquiry. The probe that ended last year confirmed the conclusions that Western governments and Russian dissidents reached long ago. The presiding judge, Sir Robert Owen, found that the FSB killed Litvinenko on orders from the highest levels of the Russian state, "probably" including Putin himself, according to Owen's report.

The 329-page report detailed the extremes to which Russian spies were capable of going in the heart of the West. The killers used a devastatingly lethal poison of a kind that is manufactured in secret Russian government labs, according to the report. The physical effect on the victim was comparable to ingesting a tiny nuclear bomb. The symbolic effect was to send a mocking message to the world about the impunity of the masterminds, since there was a good chance that the cause of death would be discovered and connected to Moscow.

Because the brutish assassins apparently did not know they'd been given polonium, they left radioactive trails across Europe during three separate missions to London, failing in their first attempt to kill Litvinenko by slipping the poison into his drink, according to the report. Although British prosecutors charged the duo with murder and sought extradition, the suspects remain free in Russia. One of them, KGB veteran Andrei Lugovoi, was elected to the Russian parliament in 2007. (Both men, and the Kremlin, deny the charges.)

The relationship between Moscow and London has never recovered, according to officials and experts in Britain and elsewhere. The scope of Russian spying in Europe has escalated steadily and dramatically, Western security officials and diplomats say. After shifting much of their energy to fighting Islamic terrorism in the early 2000s, European counterintelligence agencies have been forced to redeploy personnel and resources to confront the Russian threat.

"The spy-versus-spy activity with the Russians is very intense," the senior French intelligence official said. "And occasionally we expel them, or give them a tap on the shoulder and tell them to cut it out. These matters are often resolved service to service, rather than through prosecuting people. The FSB still cooperates well with us on antiterrorism, even if we know their partner agencies are trying to pick our pockets and steal secrets."

The cloak-and-dagger duel occasionally has an old-school air. Last May, a plainclothes team of Italian police detectives arrested two men meeting in a small café in the riverfront Trastevere area of Rome. The two had been under surveillance by Portuguese counterintelligence officers and other Western spy services for some time.

One suspect was Frederico Carvalho Gil, then 57, a veteran of Portugal's spy agency. The other was identified as Sergey Nicolaevich Pozdnyakov, 48, described by European national security officials as a senior officer in the SVR, Russia's foreign intelligence service. He had once been stationed in Italy, but was allegedly operating as an "illegal" — a spy without diplomatic cover — when he was caught. He was accused of serving as a handler for Carvalho, paying him to obtain secret intelligence related to NATO, according to Italian and Portuguese authorities.

The investigation indicated the Portuguese intelligence officer had drifted into a "double life" after a difficult divorce, according to the Corriere della Sera newspaper. Carvalho allegedly had relationships with Eastern European women and posted references on social media about his travels in Russia, according to the Corriere.

Italian police say Carvalho went to Rome to slip his handler NATO documents in exchange for 10,000 euros in cash, one of a series of such meetings in Italy and elsewhere. Still, the contents of the secret papers confiscated in Rome seemed relatively "banal" for a Russian spy to expose himself to possible capture, an Italian national security official told ProPublica.

Carvalho, who has denied the charges, awaits trial in Portugal. Italian authorities held the Russian, then sent him back to Moscow after an appeals court rejected an extradition request from Portugal.

Russian operatives take surprising risks, according to European and U.S. officials. The attempted coup in Montenegro last year is a case in point.

Montenegro, a strategically situated Balkan nation with a population of only 600,000, applied to join NATO last May. Russia lobbied strenuously against the impending membership, using diplomatic and non-governmental resources including the Orthodox Church. Russian agents stirred up protests against NATO and funded busloads of demonstrators.

Then came an uproar. Montenegro prosecutors charged that two Russian spies and two Serbian nationalists plotted last October to deploy a band of gunmen to assassinate the prime minister, storm Parliament and install an anti-NATO government. The accused spies, one of whom had previously been expelled from Poland, eluded capture. The Serbians are being prosecuted. A complex investigation continues, but Western officials say they have obtained information confirming Montenegro's charges that Russian spies attempted the overthrow of a European government.

"The thesis is they escalated to that level because the Russian government was not happy with the way Montenegro was going," a U.S. official said. "They were unhappy with the inability of their people operating on the ground to influence politics."

If the Montenegro plot showed a willingness to resort to brute force, Russia-watchers say the larger strategy features more high-tech methods, such as the mix of cyberattacks and information leaks during the U.S. elections.

"Hacking is another tool in the toolbox," the U.S. official said. "This appears to be trending toward state sponsorship and involvement. This is what worries us. The use of state power, intelligence and other methods, to affect the democratic process in European nations."

Russia is not alone in using cyberwarfare, but it is the only nation to have combined it with conventional warfare, according to Foxall, the scholar at the London think tank. Such hybrid offensives took place during Russia's war with Georgia in 2008 and its annexation of Crimea in 2014, he said.

Nations outside Russia's buffer zone have not been immune, according to experts and Western officials. During the past few years, experts and officials say, suspected Russian hackers have penetrated targets including the Italian foreign ministry; the Warsaw stock exchange; a German steel mill; the European Parliament; and the computer files of a Dutch air safety team investigating a missile attack by pro-Russian fighters that downed Malaysia Airlines Flight 17 over Ukraine in 2014, killing 298 people.

"If you think of all these incidents as a whole, you reach a worrisome conclusion," Foxall said.

The crippling hack of France TV5 Monde sent a clear message. It took place in April 2015 amid tension in Europe about the intertwined threats of Islamic terrorism and an influx of hundreds of thousands of migrants into

Greece, many of them refugees fleeing Russian-backed military onslaughts in Syria.

On the day of the cyberattack, two French government ministers visited the headquarters of the network, which airs 11 channels and broadcasts in Belgium, Switzerland, Canada and other Francophone nations, to celebrate the launch of a new channel. The hackers took over the network's programming and social media accounts, filling screens with Islamic jihadi propaganda. It took the network hours to regain control of its broadcasts and prevent its systems from being destroyed.

The hackers had breached TV5's defenses via its email messaging networks months earlier, according to Nicolas Arpagian, a French cybersecurity expert affiliated with government think tanks. Although the hackers claimed allegiance to a "CyberCaliphate," the investigation points at culprits linked to the Russian state, according to Arpagian and Western officials.

"The goal seems to have been destabilization," Arpagian said. "A demonstration of capability, of the potential to disrupt."

Definitive proof of Russian state involvement is elusive, however. Experts say the Kremlin's 21st century approach to what the Soviets once called "active measures," combines cyber-operations with the overt continuum of fake news, internet "trolling," and state-controlled media.

The strategy emerged in response to the anti-Kremlin "color revolutions" of the early 2000s, when throngs of ordinary citizens took to the streets to demand the ouster of Moscow-backed leaders in Ukraine and

Georgia, experts say. Russian leaders believed the United States was using "soft power" means, such as the media and diplomacy, to cause trouble in Russia's domain. The Russians decided to develop a comparable capacity. But the result wasn't soft very long, especially as the Kremlin became concerned that events such as the Arab Spring could spark unrest in Russia, experts say.

"The logic of influence and projection overseas was replaced by the concept of 'confrontation with the West' and the image of a 'besieged fortress,'" wrote Céline Marangé of France's Institute for Strategic Research at the Military Academy, in a study this year. "Without completely disappearing, the notion of soft power has been eclipsed by that of "information war," whose acceptance is literal and extensive in Russia. In Russian defense and security circles … and in numerous prime-time television debates, there is an almost unanimous thesis: a worldwide 'information war' at the global level pits Russia, like the Soviet Union in its day, against the West."

The combatants range from teams of "trolls" in warehouses who bombard selected targets on social media to provincial journalists who concoct wild tales following general directives rather than explicit orders, according to experts and intelligence officials. Putin's government is presented as the lone guardian of traditional Christian values fighting barbaric Muslim hordes and a soft, decadent West. The relentless narrative: Europe is under assault by crime, Muslims, terrorism, immigration, homosexuality, political correctness and effete bureaucrats.

Occasionally, fake news stories go viral and flood into the venues such as the Russian-backed RT television network and the Sputnik news agency, whose slick content reaches an increasing audience in Europe and the United States.

One example: the horrifying tale of "Lisa," a Russian-German teenager who told police she was kidnapped and raped by three men resembling Muslim immigrants. The case erupted in January of last year. Europe was on edge because of the very real and ugly spate of sexual assaults on women by groups of men, many of them of Muslim descent, during New Year's Eve celebrations in Cologne, Germany.

The German authorities insisted from the beginning that there was no proof of the girl's allegations. But the Lisa story gained momentum, driven by heavy, sometimes inaccurate coverage on Kremlin-backed and pro-Russian outlets as well as social media. The frenzy reached the point that Russia's foreign minister, Sergey Lavrov, said at a news conference that German authorities appeared to be hushing up the incident out of political correctness, according to news reports.

Soon, however, the teenager admitted to lying. She had stayed overnight at the home of a 19-year-old male friend without permission and invented the rape story to explain her disappearance, according to media reports.

There is no evidence Russian operatives played a role in creating the initial story. But the German government and other critics have rebuked the Kremlin and the Russian media, saying they amplified and distorted the case even after it was shown to be untrue.

"The story was totally fake," Foxall said. "This is a well-established pattern. Other stories have travelled such a path, but without the same kind of success."

THE NEW COLD WAR

Nonetheless, Russian influence campaigns find a more welcoming political atmosphere in Europe than in the United States. After all, leftist parties in France, Italy and other nations had strong ideological and financial ties to the Soviet Union during the Cold War. There is also a pro-Russian tradition, often fomented by anti-Americanism, among some rightist and nationalist parties.

Russia spends considerable money and energy wooing sympathetic European politicians and activists. They are often, though not always, populist, nationalist, fascist, far-left, anti-system or just plain disruptive. The most powerful unabashedly pro-Moscow figure is probably Le Pen, whose presidential campaign has thrived partly because of her effort to distance herself from the angry, anti-Semitic image of her father, National Front founder Jean-Marie Le Pen.

The list also includes Nigel Farage, the brash British politician who oversaw the underdog campaign for the Brexit, and admires both President Putin and President Trump; Nick Griffin of the far-right British National Party, who after observing Russian legislative elections in 2011 pronounced them "much fairer than Britain's"; and Matteo Salvini of the rightist and separatist Lega Nord (Northern League), which along with the populist 5 Stelle party constitutes a large pro-Moscow bloc in Italy.

To be sure, more moderate leaders in Europe also favor stronger ties to Russia and have good relationships with President Putin. Among them is former French Prime Minister François Fillon, the center-right presidential candidate competing for a spot in the runoff election.

Russian officials and their European allies argue that Moscow's legitimate diplomatic outreach is being demonized. But European government officials worry about activity that crosses the line into funding, recruitment and manipulation by spy agencies.

"I think some of our political parties are vulnerable to infiltration," the Italian national security official said. "They don't have the experience, the anti-bodies, to fend off such formidable intelligence services."

And there are concerns about wider repercussions. In January, the Center for International Research at Sciences Po, one of France's most prestigious universities, abruptly canceled a scheduled appearance in Paris by David Satter, an American author. Satter is a well-regarded foreign correspondent who has spent four decades covering Russia. In 2013, he became the first U.S. journalist expelled from the country by the Kremlin since the Cold War. His latest book, "The Less You Know, The Better You Sleep," details allegations that Russian intelligence services were covertly involved in mass-casualty terrorist attacks in Russia.

The cancellation caused a fierce debate about censorship when a leaked email revealed that administrators made the decision because they feared reprisals against Sciences Po students and researchers in Russia, citing the "current context of tensions," according to Le Monde newspaper.

Despite the tensions in Europe and the concerns about interference, recent elections in the Netherlands went off without problems, with the party Moscow favored running well behind. The next test will be Sunday's vote in France, where cybersecurity agencies are on alert. The government has taken precautions such as requiring the estimated 1.8 million French voters living overseas to cast their ballots by mail or proxy, rather than online, according to French officials.

"What we have seen so far is enough to conclude that the Russians have carried out an influence campaign," a French diplomat said. "But I don't think it will have a significant impact on the outcome of the election. We have to stay calm."

1. Explain how Russia has been involved in European and US elections.

2. What does the author suggest this means for democracy? What are Russia's intentions with election involvement?

CHAPTER 2

WHAT THE GOVERNMENT AND POLITICIANS SAY

Although the Cold War played out on many fronts, it was by and large a political conflict. Politicians in the Soviet Union and the United States responded to and played into tensions between the two countries, and policy was shaped in both countries based on the conflict. Today, a similar political dynamic is developing between the United States and Russia, with political figures responding to questions about tension between the countries while also making policy decisions in the context of growing conflict. The goals of a new Cold War dynamic are also largely political; undermining the influence of either country is the simplified goal of both nations. This means that statements by politicians carry particular weight, both at home and on the international stage.

EXCERPT FROM "DECLASSIFIED INTELLIGENCE COMMUNITY ASSESSMENT OF RUSSIAN ACTIVITIES AND INTENTIONS IN RECENT U.S. ELECTIONS," FROM THE OFFICE OF THE DIRECTOR OF NATIONAL INTELLIGENCE, JANUARY 6, 2017

ASSESSING RUSSIAN ACTIVITIES AND INTENTIONS IN RECENT US ELECTIONS

KEY JUDGMENTS

Russian efforts to influence the 2016 US presidential election represent the most recent expression of Moscow's longstanding desire to undermine the US-led liberal democratic order, but these activities demonstrated a significant escalation in directness, level of activity, and scope of effort compared to previous operations.

We assess Russian President Vladimir Putin ordered an influence campaign in 2016 aimed at the US presidential election. Russia's goals were to undermine public faith in the US democratic process, denigrate Secretary Clinton, and harm her electability and potential presidency. We further assess Putin and the Russian Government developed a clear preference for President-elect Trump. We have high confidence in these judgments.

- We also assess Putin and the Russian Government aspired to help President-elect Trump's election chances when possible by discrediting Secretary

Clinton and publicly contrasting her unfavorably to him. All three agencies agree with this judgment. CIA and FBI have high confidence in this judgment; NSA has moderate confidence.

- Moscow's approach evolved over the course of the campaign based on Russia's understanding of the electoral prospects of the two main candidates. When it appeared to Moscow that Secretary Clinton was likely to win the election, the Russian influence campaign began to focus more on undermining her future presidency.
- Further information has come to light since Election Day that, when combined with Russian behavior since early November 2016, increases our confidence in our assessments of Russian motivations and goals.

Moscow's influence campaign followed a Russian messaging strategy that blends covert intelligence operations—such as cyber activity—with overt efforts by Russian Government agencies, state-funded media, third-party intermediaries, and paid social media users or "trolls." Russia, like its Soviet predecessor, has a history of conducting covert influence campaigns focused on US presidential elections that have used intelligence officers and agents and press placements to disparage candidates perceived as hostile to the Kremlin.

- Russia's intelligence services conducted cyber operations against targets associated with the 2016 US presidential election, including targets associated with both major US political parties.
- We assess with high confidence that Russian military intelligence (General Staff Main Intelligence Directorate

or GRU) used the Guccifer 2.0 persona and DCLeaks.com to release US victim data obtained in cyber operations publicly and in exclusives to media outlets and relayed material to WikiLeaks.

- Russian intelligence obtained and maintained access to elements of multiple US state or local electoral boards. DHS assesses that the types of systems Russian actors targeted or compromised were not involved in vote tallying.
- Russia's state-run propaganda machine contributed to the influence campaign by serving as a platform for Kremlin messaging to Russian and international audiences.

We assess Moscow will apply lessons learned from its Putin-ordered campaign aimed at the US presidential election to future influence efforts worldwide, including against US allies and their election processes.

1. What involvement by the Russians has the intelligence community found in the 2016 election?

2. What are some of the possible ramifications of the sort of interference the Russians are suspected of?

"THE ADMINISTRATION'S RESPONSE TO RUSSIA: WHAT YOU NEED TO KNOW," BY NED PRICE, FROM THE WHITE HOUSE ARCHIVES, DECEMBER 29, 2016

Today, President Obama authorized a number of actions in response to the Russian government's aggressive harassment of U.S. officials and cyber operations aimed at the U.S. election in 2016. Russia's cyber activities were intended to influence the election, erode faith in U.S. democratic institutions, sow doubt about the integrity of our electoral process, and undermine confidence in the institutions of the U.S. government. These actions are unacceptable and will not be tolerated.

The President released the following statement regarding today's actions:

"Today, I have ordered a number of actions in response to the Russian government's aggressive harassment of U.S. officials and cyber operations aimed at the U.S. election. These actions follow repeated private and public warnings that we have issued to the Russian government, and are a necessary and appropriate response to efforts to harm U.S. interests in violation of established international norms of behavior.

All Americans should be alarmed by Russia's actions. In October, my Administration publicized our assessment that Russia took actions intended to interfere with the U.S. election process. These data theft and disclosure activities could only have been directed by the highest levels of the Russian government. Moreover, our diplomats have experienced an unacceptable level of harassment in Moscow by Russian security services and police over the last year. Such activities have consequences. Today, I have ordered a number of actions in response.

I have issued an executive order that provides additional authority for responding to certain cyber activity that seeks to interfere with or undermine our election processes and institutions, or those of our allies or partners. Using this new authority, I have sanctioned nine entities and individuals: the GRU and the FSB, two Russian intelligence services; four individual officers of the GRU; and three companies that provided material support to the GRU's cyber operations. In addition, the Secretary of the Treasury is designating two Russian individuals for using cyber-enabled means to cause misappropriation of funds and personal identifying information.

The State Department is also shutting down two Russian compounds, in Maryland and New York, used by Russian personnel for intelligence-related purposes, and is declaring "persona non grata" 35 Russian intelligence operatives. Finally, the Department of Homeland Security and the Federal Bureau of Investigation are releasing declassified technical information on Russian civilian and military intelligence service cyber activity, to help network defenders in the United States and abroad identify, detect, and disrupt Russia's global campaign of malicious cyber activities.

These actions are not the sum total of our response to Russia's aggressive activities. We will continue to take a variety of actions at a time and place of our choosing, some of which will not be publicized. In addition to holding Russia accountable for what it has done, the United States and friends and allies around the world must work together to oppose Russia's efforts to undermine established international norms of behavior, and interfere with democratic governance. To that end, my Administration will be providing a report to Congress in the coming days about Russia's efforts to interfere in our election, as well as malicious cyber activity related to our election cycle in previous elections."

HERE ARE SOME OF THE WAYS IN WHICH PRESIDENT OBAMA IS TAKING ACTION:

SANCTIONING MALICIOUS RUSSIAN CYBER ACTIVITY

In response to the threat to U.S. national security posed by Russian interference in our elections, the President has approved an amendment to Executive Order 13964. As originally issued in April 2015, this Executive Order created a new, targeted authority for the U.S. government to respond more effectively to the most significant of cyber threats, particularly in situations where malicious cyber actors operate beyond the reach of existing authorities. The original Executive Order focused on cyber-enabled malicious activities that:

- Harm or significantly compromise the provision of services by entities in a critical infrastructure sector;
- Significantly disrupt the availability of a computer or network of computers (for example, through a distributed denial-of-service attack); or
- Cause a significant misappropriation of funds or economic resources, trade secrets, personal identifiers, or financial information for commercial or competitive advantage or private financial gain (for example, by stealing large quantities of credit card information, trade secrets, or sensitive information).

RESPONDING TO RUSSIAN HARASSMENT OF U.S. PERSONNEL

Over the past two years, harassment of our diplomatic personnel in Russia by security personnel and police has increased significantly and gone far beyond international diplomatic norms of behavior. Other Western Embassies have reported similar concerns. In response to this harassment, the President has authorized the following actions:

Today the State Department declared 35 Russian government officials from the Russian Embassy in Washington and the Russian Consulate in San Francisco "persona non grata." They were acting in a manner inconsistent with their diplomatic status. Those individuals and their families were given 72 hours to leave the United States.

In addition to this action, the Department of State has provided notice that as of noon on Friday, December 30, Russian access will be denied to two Russian government-owned compounds, one in Maryland and one in New York.

RAISING AWARENESS ABOUT RUSSIAN MALICIOUS CYBER ACTIVITY

The Department of Homeland Security and Federal Bureau of Investigation are releasing a Joint Analysis Report (JAR) that contains declassified technical information on Russian civilian and military intelligence services' malicious cyber activity, to better help network defenders in the United States and abroad identify, detect, and disrupt Russia's global campaign of malicious cyber activities.

- The JAR includes information on computers around the world that Russian intelligence services have co-opted without the knowledge of their owners in order to conduct their malicious activity in a way that makes it difficult to trace back to Russia. In some cases, the cybersecurity community was aware of this infrastructure, in other cases, this information is newly declassified by the U.S. government.
- The report also includes data that enables cyber security firms and other network defenders to identify certain malware that the Russian intelligence services use. Network defenders can use this information to identify and block Russian malware, forcing the Russian intelligence services to re-engineer their malware. This information is newly de-classified.
- Finally, the JAR includes information on how Russian intelligence services typically conduct their activities. This information can help network defenders better identify new tactics or techniques that a malicious actor might deploy or detect and disrupt an ongoing intrusion.

57

As the Administration stated today, cyber threats pose one of the most serious economic and national security challenges the United States faces today. For the last eight years, this Administration has pursued a comprehensive strategy to confront these threats. And as we have demonstrated by these actions today, we intend to continue to employ the full range of authorities and tools, including diplomatic engagement, trade policy tools, and law enforcement mechanisms, to counter the threat posed by malicious cyber actors, regardless of their country of origin, to protect the national security of the United States.

1. Why did the United States choose to sanction Russia?

2. What were some of the actions taken by President Obama in response to Russia?

"STATEMENT BY THE PRESIDENT ON ACTIONS IN RESPONSE TO RUSSIAN MALICIOUS CYBER ACTIVITY AND HARASSMENT," FROM THE WHITE HOUSE ARCHIVES (PRESIDENT BARACK OBAMA), DECEMBER 29, 2016

Today, I have ordered a number of actions in response to the Russian government's aggressive harassment of U.S. officials and cyber operations aimed at the U.S. election.

These actions follow repeated private and public warnings that we have issued to the Russian government, and are a necessary and appropriate response to efforts to harm U.S. interests in violation of established international norms of behavior.

All Americans should be alarmed by Russia's actions. In October, my Administration publicized our assessment that Russia took actions intended to interfere with the U.S. election process. These data theft and disclosure activities could only have been directed by the highest levels of the Russian government. Moreover, our diplomats have experienced an unacceptable level of harassment in Moscow by Russian security services and police over the last year. Such activities have consequences. Today, I have ordered a number of actions in response.

I have issued an executive order that provides additional authority for responding to certain cyber activity that seeks to interfere with or undermine our election processes and institutions, or those of our allies or partners. Using this new authority, I have sanctioned nine entities and individuals: the GRU and the FSB, two Russian intelligence services; four individual officers of the GRU; and three companies that provided material support to the GRU's cyber operations. In addition, the Secretary of the Treasury is designating two Russian individuals for using cyber-enabled means to cause misappropriation of funds and personal identifying information. The State Department is also shutting down two Russian compounds, in Maryland and New York, used by Russian personnel for intelligence-related purposes, and is declaring "persona non grata" 35 Russian intelligence operatives. Finally, the Department of Homeland Security and the Federal Bureau of Investigation are releasing declassified technical information on Russian civilian and military intelligence service cyber activity, to help network defenders in the United States and abroad identify, detect, and disrupt Russia's global campaign of malicious cyber activities.

These actions are not the sum total of our response to Russia's aggressive activities. We will continue to take a variety of actions at a time and place of our choosing, some of which will not be publicized. In addition to holding Russia accountable for what it has done, the United States and friends and allies around the world must work together to oppose Russia's efforts to undermine established international norms of behavior, and interfere with democratic governance. To that end, my Administration will be providing a report to Congress in the coming days about Russia's efforts to interfere in our election, as well as malicious cyber activity related to our election cycle in previous elections.

1. Explain Russia's cyber activity and why the United States chose to respond.

2. Describe this statement in the context of a "new Cold War." Does it sound diplomatic or does it suggest increasing tension?

"STATEMENT BY THE PRESIDENT ON NEW SANCTIONS RELATED TO RUSSIA," FROM THE WHITE HOUSE ARCHIVES (PRESIDENT BARACK OBAMA), SEPTEMBER 11, 2014

Today, we join the European Union in announcing that we will intensify our coordinated sanctions on Russia in response to its illegal actions in Ukraine. I have said from the very beginning of this crisis that we want to see a negotiated political solution that respects Ukraine's sovereignty and territorial integrity. Together with G-7 and European partners and our other Allies, we have made clear that we are prepared to impose mounting costs on Russia. We are implementing these new measures in light of Russia's actions to further destabilize Ukraine over the last month, including through the presence of heavily armed Russian forces in eastern Ukraine. We are watching closely developments since the announcement of the ceasefire and agreement in Minsk, but we have yet to see conclusive evidence that Russia has ceased its efforts to destabilize Ukraine.

We will deepen and broaden sanctions in Russia's financial, energy, and defense sectors. These measures will increase Russia's political isolation as well as the economic costs to Russia, especially in areas of importance to President Putin and those close to him. My Administration will outline the specifics of these new sanctions tomorrow.

The international community continues to seek a genuine negotiated solution to the crisis in Ukraine. I encourage President Putin to work with Ukraine and other international partners, within the context of the Minsk agreement and without setting unreasonable conditions, to reach a lasting resolution to the conflict. As I said last week, if Russia fully implements its commitments, these sanctions can be rolled back. If, instead, Russia continues its aggressive actions and violations of international law, the costs will continue to rise.

1. Who has the United States partnered with on these sanctions?

2. Why would the United States sanction Russia over actions in another country?

"TENSIONS RISE AS RUSSIA RETALIATES AGAINST NEW SANCTIONS BILL," BY JULIA CONLEY, FROM *COMMON DREAMS*, JULY 28, 2017

Members of the U.S. diplomatic staff in Russia will be expelled in the coming weeks, following an order on Friday by the Russian Foreign Ministry. The move was made in response to a new economic sanctions bill that passed in both houses of the U.S. Congress.

Russia said it would also seize two properties used by the U.S. Embassy by next week. Reuters cited a report by Russia's Interfax news agency saying "hundreds" of employees would be affected, by the exact number was not clear.

The legislation, meant to retaliate against Russia for its alleged interference in the 2016 election, passed in a vote of 419 to 3 on Thursday, effectively veto-proofing the bill should President Donald Trump want to overrule it. The White House has said in recent weeks that it didn't want new sanctions in place. The Obama administration imposed earlier sanctions late last year just after the election.

White House Press Secretary Sarah Huckabee Sanders said Thursday that Trump would review the bill and that she didn't know whether he would sign it, but the Kremlin said that Russia had announced their plan to retaliate without waiting for Trump's decision, because "technically the form passed by the Senate is more important."

The new sanctions would impact the Russian energy and financial sectors, and the European Union has expressed concerns that they could also affect European companies involved in the building of a new pipeline from Germany to Russia.

On Thursday, Russian President Vladimir Putin said he "very much regrets" the strained relations between the U.S. and Russia, and accused the U.S. of displaying "boorish behavior" and "anti-Russia hysteria."

The Russian foreign ministry called allegations that it meddled in the 2016 election "an absolutely invented pretext."

Tensions between the U.S. and Russia have deepened since the election, despite a relatively warm relationship between Trump and Putin. In addition to an on-camera meeting, the two leaders spoke privately at the G20 Summit earlier this month, in a meeting that was initially undisclosed. News of the talk came in the wake of reports that Donald Trump, Jr., met with a Russian lawyer during the 2016 campaign after being told he could gather damaging information about Hillary Clinton in the meeting.

While the Trump administration has dismissed much of the coverage of the issue as "fake news," Russian officials have continued to deny involvement in the hacking of Democratic Party emails or efforts to swing the election.

1. How has the Trump administration characterized Russian alleged involvement in the 2016 election?

2. Explain the bill discussed in this piece and what the possible ramifications of it might be.

"VICE PRESIDENT BIDEN'S REMARKS AT MOSCOW STATE UNIVERSITY," FROM THE WHITE HOUSE ARCHIVES, MARCH 10, 2011

THE VICE PRESIDENT: Thank you, Andy. Rector, thank you. It's an honor to be here at Moscow State University. And I want to thank the AmCham chamber for sponsoring this.

To the students that are here, I apologize. In America, we have a rule. You don't have to wait any longer than 20 minutes for a full professor. And for someone who is not a full professor, you need only wait 10 minutes. I'm honored you waited at all. I do apologize to the business community, as well as the students, for keeping you waiting.

I want to publicly as well thank President Medvedev and Prime Minister Putin for their hospitality. We have very good meetings, very long meetings, and I hope, productive.

And I want to thank AmCham Russia for sponsoring this event, working to foster a modern business climate after the fall of communism.

And, Rector, again, thank you for hosting us here at Moscow State University, which has given Russia and the world so many and such an extraordinary array of graduates, among them eight-- if I'm not mistaken, eight Nobel Laureates, including former President Gorbachev, who I have known for some time.

In addition to my wife, Jill, I brought along my granddaughter. Her name is -- my number two granddaughter. Her name is Finnegan Biden. And I brought her along to Russia, because I wanted her to see this great country with her own eyes, the country of Pushkin's poetry and Tolstoy's prose, the country of Tchaikovsky's compositions, and Zhukov's and Gagarin's heroic feats. It is a rich and a noble culture. And I'm delighted she has had a chance to get a -- just a little glimpse of it.

Let me also thank our Ambassador John Beyrle, and his team, for hosting me. As you businesspeople know, there's an old expression if you're in the military -- but also if you're in the diplomatic corps. The good news is the commanding general is coming. The bad news is the commanding general is coming. On the diplomatic side, the good news is the Vice President is coming, and the bad news, the Vice President is coming because I've created an extraordinary amount of work for John's incredible team.

But John is one of the best America has to offer. And anyone who doubts the ability of Americans and Russians to work together, need only examine the history of John's family. His father, Joe -- Joseph was a hero in both Russia and the United States, an American soldier taken prisoner by the Nazis who went on -- later when he escaped to fight with the Red Army on the Eastern Front. And now, more than 65 years later, his son is the American envoy to Moscow. I think that's a remarkable, remarkable story.

And today, I also want to address -- and the main reason I'm here -- is the state of U.S.-Russian relations. I don't need to tell anyone in this audience that our administration, when we took office in January of '09, our relationship with Russia had hit a fairly low point that had accumulated over the previous eight years.

Yes, so we saw a war between Russia and Georgia played out, and played a role in that decline. But even before that conflict erupted in August of '08, a dangerous drift was underway in this important relationship. While we no longer considered each other enemies, we couldn't always tell from the rhetoric that was flying back and forth across the continent.

Ironically, this came at a time when American and Russian interests -- on nuclear arms control, nonproliferation, stabilizing Afghanistan, fighting terrorism, opening global markets and a range of other issues -- at a time when all of them, we were more closely aligned than ever on each and every one of those issues.

So to seize this opportunity, President Obama and I proposed forging a fresh new start by, as I said in the initial speech on our foreign policy, by pressing a restart button, reset button. We wanted to literally reset this relationship, reset it in a way that reflected our mutual interests, so that our countries could move forward together.

The President asked me to make that "reset" the focus of our administration's first foreign policy speech, that I delivered several weeks after our inauguration at the Munich Security Conference. And I said then, and I quote, "the United States and Russia can disagree and still -- still -- work together where our interests coincide. And they coincide in many places."

Now, we know that pursuing this agenda -- we knew pursuing this agenda would be hard work, that old habits -- as we say in America, old habits die hard. That's why President Obama has met nearly a dozen times with President Medvedev, and why together we established a Bilateral Presidential Commission with working groups on key issues like arms control and energy, broadening the contacts between our two governments.

And in spite, in spite of what we call -- excuse me, in the spirit of what we call in America a "dual-track engagement," we've also worked to deepen our ties between our countries' business leaders, including many of the distinguished men and women in this room, as well as between our civil society groups.

Our business and civil society summits, alongside our presidential summits in 2009 and 2010, were in my view very important in strengthening these relationships. We believed then, and still believe, in focusing on concrete outcomes that serve both countries' interests, as President Obama puts it, "win-win," situations.

And we reject -- we reject, the President and I -- the tired theory that our values and our interests must compete for influence over our politics. We flat reject that notion because we believe and we will continue to stand up for our principles. And I believe those principles make all of us, Americans and Russians alike, more secure, more prosperous, and more free.

Two years since we pressed that reset button, I would argue the benefits of this approach to both our countries are absolutely clear on issue after issue.

Arms control: We signed and ratified a New START Treaty, which will reduce our deployment of strategic weapons while ensuring that we maintain stable and predictable verification.

The two countries with the largest nuclear arsenals showed the world that they are serious about arms control and strengthening global nonproliferation. And that gave us even more credibility to deal with the most egregious violators of their international commitments.

Iran: With our partners in the so called P5 plus 1, we -- Russia and the United States -- gave Tehran a chance for meaningful dialogue based on mutual interests and mutual respect to develop peaceful nuclear means. They simply rejected it. So Russia and the United States, along with our partners on the U.N. Security Council, adopted what is known as Resolution 1929, the most extensive package of sanctions Iran has ever faced.

And Moscow, on its own and to its own -- as costing it in dollars and rubles -- Moscow took another important step: It canceled its contract to sell to Iran S-300, air-defense missile systems, which was an unambiguous sign -- an unambiguous sign -- of international resolve that Iran must address the concerns that we have over their nuclear program.

North Korea -- working closely with Russia and our other international partners on the threat posed by

Pyongyang, we adopted another U.N. resolution, referred as 1874, which authorized inspections -- almost unprecedented, authorized inspections of vessels -- Korean vessels -- suspected of carrying nuclear materials into or out of their country. And the nations of the world have cooperated.

I would argue it's because Russia and the United States were leading in this effort.

Afghanistan -- we're cooperating on what we call the Northern Distribution Network, which now brings vital supplies to the ISAF, International Security Forces, including American soldiers and civilians into Afghanistan. In addition to rail cars rolling through Russia with supplies, over 800 flights have carried nearly 120,000 passengers over Russian territory to Afghanistan. That would have been thought impossible four years ago.

And Russia is also providing badly needed military equipment and training to the Afghan National Security Forces. We're also cooperating on drug eradication.

European security -- using America's improved relationship with Russia as a model, we also reset relations between Russia and NATO during last year's Lisbon Summit, and a great deal of credit goes to President Medvedev. And we identified missile defense as a common project.

I've talked extensively with your leaders on this issue. It will be difficult, but it will be a game-changer if we can get it done. It will say to the world, the two largest superpowers in the world are mutually developing the ability to have missile defenses, which I would argue would have an extremely important impact on dissuading so many of the countries who are contemplating becoming nuclear powers from doing so.

This year, we'll seek agreement on an ambitious work plan for cooperation on this once contentious issue. And we'll also pursue an agreement on negotiations to modernize and strengthen the Conventional Forces in Europe Treaty. I've been around a long time -- the CFE Treaty has been something we've been working on since the late '70s. We have an opportunity to make more progress.

Central Asia -- we're working together to foster a stable -- a stable, democratic government -- a stable, democratic government -- and I might add a great deal of the credit goes to your President -- in Kyrgyzstan, combating drug traffickers, eradicating polio -- steps that suggest we can move beyond the so-called "Grand Game" and "spheres of influence," a Cold War relic in my view.

Cooperation on each of these important issues has made America more secure -- and I would argue, presumptuous of me, but I believe it's made Russia more secure.

But the reset has also produced more subtle signs of progress, again ones that would not have been contemplated even four years ago. Russian helicopters used for relief efforts in Sudan. California firefighters helping to fight wildfires in central Russia. American and Russian drug officers working side-by-side in Afghanistan, the world's largest producer of heroin and opium as a consequence of it. Student body presidents from American universities discussing democracy and human rights with Kremlin advisors. And we're very pleased that are here today in the audience.

These things clearly would have been hard to imagine amid the mistrust and ill will a little over two years ago. And to some of you, they may sound small. But having been involved in this relationship for over 36 years, they are more than the sum of their parts.

And if you think I'm exaggerating and overstating the case, consider the following statistics -- or polling. In

December of 2008 -- December of 2008, one month before we were sworn in as President and Vice President, polling showed that only 17 percent of all Russians had a positive opinion of the United States -- 17 percent. This year, that number has jumped to over 60 percent. Our goal is to have it continue to climb.

That same year, Americans ranked Russia as one of the top five countries threatening American security -- two years ago. This year, only 2 percent of the entire American population say they view Russia as a threat. All of this leads to one very important conclusion in the mind of one Vice President that I think is now beyond dispute: the reset is working. Working for all of us, working for Russia. And I would presumptuously suggest working for the world.

But there is still, still much work to be done to enhance our security cooperation and our closeness.

On the Caucasus -- we have a genuine disagreement not only with your leadership but with the vast majority of the Russian people over Georgia. But there's a larger principle at stake here in our view -- and I want to be straightforward because if friends cannot be straightforward with friends, it really isn't friendship based on mutual trust.

We think there's a larger principle at stake here. As I said when I announced the reset at Munich I said, "It will remain our view that sovereign states have the right to make their own decisions and choose their own alliances."

And further: "We will not recognize any state having a sphere of influence." And almost regardless of the difficulty, we don't support any state deciding through force changing the leadership of an elected -- democratically elected individual.

We have also worked closely, though, with both Russia and Georgia to reduce the threat of further conflict. As a result, Georgia recently restarted its commitment -- restated its commitment to non-use of first use of -- non-use of force, and commercial flights have resumed between Moscow and Tbilisi. But we must do more to assist those displaced by the 2008 conflict and enable normal travel and commerce to occur.

Our joint diplomacy was essential and is essential in ending conflicts in other areas. Excuse me -- Nagorno-Karabakh, where I would again commend President Medvedev for his tireless work for a peaceful and permanent settlement there.

But the next frontier in our relationship -- and the main area in my view and the President of the United States' view of future opportunities and challenges -- will be building stronger ties of trade and commerce that match the security cooperation we have accomplished over the last two years and hopefully will continue to grow.

In the 20th Century, the wealth of a nation was measured by the abundance of its natural resources, the expanse of its landmass or the size of its army. Russia had all of those things.

But in the 21st Century, the true wealth of a nation is found in the creative minds of its people and their ability to innovate. There, too, Russia is remarkably blessed. Unleashing Russia's full potential will be a boon and an opportunity not only for the United States and for Russians, but again for international commerce and peace and justice.

Already, our economic relationship is moving to center stage. Pepsico has made a multi-billion dollar investment in Russia -- Russia's leading juice and dietary producer. Imagine five years ago, the likelihood that an American company could buy, in effect, the largest of anything in Russia.

Chevron and ExxonMobil recently announced major new deals with Russian partners. General Electric is undertaking a major expansion of its operations here. And John Deere last year opened a major manufacturing center in Moscow -- in the Moscow region -- and is already -- I met with the President -- I think he may be here -- yesterday -- they're already doubling its capacity and as a consequence, employment.

And Alcoa is working closely -- very closely -- with a nanotechnology firm, Rusnano, on an array of high-tech products that are the future.

This week a coalition of public and private sector partners in Russia and the U.S. announced a new program, as well, supported by an American company, Johnson & Johnson. That program will provide pregnant women and new mothers with health information via text messages -- a great example of how civil society, government, and the private sector can work together to find innovative solutions to shared challenges -- real challenges to real people, ordinary people.

And just yesterday, I witnessed the signing of a $2 billion sale of eight Boeing 777 aircraft to Aeroflot, expanding last year's agreement to sell 50 737s to Russian Technologies. These contracts were able to be done and the plane was able to be built I might add because of Russian titanium, ingenuity and the engineers here; as well as the brilliant engineers and workface back in the United States. These contracts will create or sustain tens of thousands of jobs in Russia and in the United States.

On his visit to Silicon Valley last year, President Medvedev made clear Russia's desire to bolster our partnership in the innovation economy -- a priority the United States shares, and the President of the United States has announced as the hallmark of what we're attempting to do.

Yesterday, I had the opportunity to -- Skolkovo -- to be in Skolkovo -- a high-tech hub on the outskirts of Moscow that has the promise of becoming the Silicon Valley of Russia.

Closer cooperation will allow American companies to benefit from greater access to Russia's deep pool of talented engineers, mathematicians and computer scientists.

Mr. President, if you'll forgive me to -- I will not mention the context, but yesterday we had this discussion -- a roundtable discussion of American businesses and CEOs from Russian business. A Russian businessman said something that was true. He said the reason why it's good to be here in Russia and investing -- the United States -- is because of its market. An interesting comment from the chairman of the board of Boeing in Russia, he said, with all due respect to my good friend, that may be true, but that's not the reason we're here. Other countries have four, five, six and seven times the capacity to purchase our planes in terms of their needs. But we're here. He said let me tell you why we're here. We're here because the best engineers in the world are here. Many educated at this great university.

We're also providing -- not as a gift. When I say providing it sounds like we're providing a gift -- we're also -- American venture capitalists and other foreign investment is flowing into the Russia's economy to allow it to diversify beyond your abundant natural resources -- metals, oil and gas -- and help Russia -- Russian start-ups get their ideas to market.

Those of you who are studying business know that it's one thing to have an idea, it's another thing to get to market. It takes people willing to make a gamble, make an investment, make a bet.

Already, several of America's leading firms have shown their support for this vision, by committing to invest in the case of several venture capitalists over $1 billion dollars -- already committed -- investing in Russian high-tech industry.

But despite these steps, our trading and investment relationship is not what it should be. As a matter of fact, it was higher years ago than it is now. Russia was America's 37th largest export market in 2010. The value of the goods that cross our border, the United States border with Canada and Mexico every few days exceeds the annual value of our trade with Russia. We've got to do better. We've got to do better. And I believe we can.

This is one of the reasons the President and I so strongly support Russians accession to the World Trade Organization. Accession will enable Russia to deepen its trade relations not only with the United States, but the rest of the world. And it will give American companies a greater and more predictable -- important word, predictable -- access to Russia's growing markets, expanding both U.S. exports and employment.

The renewed energy that Russian negotiators have brought to the table in this accession effort and Moscow's political will to get the job done are for the first time in a long time genuinely moving things forward.

We're making progress on these issues that have caused so much friction in the past. We're making progress on agricultural trade, sanitary regulations, enforcement of intellectual property rights, though we still have more work to do.

So let me make this as clear as I possibly can: President Obama and I strongly support and want to see Russia in WTO. We've made that clear to the Congress; we've made that clear the world; and we've made that clear to anybody who is willing to listen.

It's better for America -- and presumptuous of me to say this, never tell another man his business or another country their interest -- but it's better for America, and I believe better for Russia to be able to trade with each other under predictable and transparent rules. And that's also why we're going to work with Congress to terminate the Jackson-Vanik amendment.

These steps are critical components to our Administration's trade agenda. There used to be a bank robber in America in the '30s. His name was Willie Sutton. And they once asked Willie Sutton, why do you rob banks, Willie. He said, that's where the money is. We're not doing Russia a favor. This is in the overall best interest, we think, of Russia, but we know for the United States. We know for our unemployment -- our employment to grow, trade, exports have to grow as well.

So we expect Russia's leaders to continue working with us to move the processes along. But you in this room know as well as anyone that even if liberalizing our trading relationship, Russia's business and legal climate quite frankly is going to have to continue to improve because right now for many companies it presents a fundamental obstacle.

In early 2008, President Medvedev described Russia as, and I quote, "a country of legal nihilism," -- not my quote, his quote -- and he prescribed a set of reforms.

The simple fact is this: Pragmatic businessmen, particularly -- and women -- particularly those who are not so big that they can go directly to each of our governments to resolve their differences -- they want to invest where they can expect a reasonable return and an absolute assurance that the legal system in the country they're investing in will provide due process.

I don't think it's reasonable to expect Americans, or Europeans, or Russians themselves, to invest confidently where -- in a country in which there are infamous cases in which property rights were violated and not protected. It may be unfair, but it is a perception.

A country in which investors -- Russian and American -- can lose when they succeed -- lose when they succeed -- in fact, have lost fortunes because of legal abuses.

A country which -- a company which can be seized, or an owner imprisoned on a politician's whim; in which a lawyer like Sergei Magnitsky -- I hope I pronounced that correctly -- can be arrested after accusing the police of fraud and then die in detention before being tried.

No amount of government cheerleading or public relations or U.S. support or rebranding will bring wronged or nervous investors back to a market they perceive to have these shortcomings. Only bold and genuine change. I'm not here to lecture. I'm not here to preach. I'm not here to tell Russia what to do. But I know from my experience, almost every country I visit, particularly smaller ones, not great countries like Russia, the first thing they'll tell me is, can you encourage, Mr. Vice President, American businesses to invest here.

And there's the same answer: Get your system right. Don't make it a gamble. Have certainty.

Over the past few months alone, our Administration has spoken out against allegations of misconduct in the trial of -- excuse me -- Khodorkovsky -- you can tell I didn't do very well in Russian -- and of the beating and detention of "Strategy 31" demonstrators.

Some of you may say, well, how can you say those things out loud, Mr. Vice President, and expect to have a better relationship. They're necessary to have a good relationship. We should not have to make choices. (Applause.) We will continue to object when we think human rights are violated or democracy and the rule of law is undermined.

For us, these are matters of principle, but I would argue they're also matters of pragmatism. History shows that in industrialized societies, economic modernization and political modernization go hand-in-hand. You don't get one without the other. Or put it this way, you don't get industrial modernization without political modernization. And I realize -- I realize -- it's been a short journey -- a short journey since, as we say in the West, the wall came down. And I realize there is an awful lot that's been accomplished. But -- but -- modernization in every way is essential.

I think that's why so many Russians now call on their country to strengthen their democratic institutions. Courts must be empowered to uphold the rule of law and protect those playing by the rules.

Non-governmental watchdogs should be applauded as patriots, not traitors. As a famous American jurist once said, a Supreme Court justice, he said, sunlight is the best disinfectant -- sunlight is the best disinfectant. In today's society, we'd probably say transparency is the best lubricant.

Journalists must be able to publish without fear of retribution. In my country it was a newspaper, not the FBI, or the Justice Department, it was a newspaper, the *Washington Post* that brought down a President for illegal actions.

Thomas Jefferson said that if he only had a choice of a free press or what we had. He said he'd choose a free press. It's the greatest guarantee of freedom there is, the so-called Third Estate. And believe me to the American press up there, they drive me crazy. It's not like they say nice things about me all the time. But I really mean it: It is the single best guarantee of political freedom.

And viable opposition -- and public parties that are able to compete is also essential to good governance. Just as competition between top athletes produces better players and better teams, it's also true that that works as well among firms who provide better services and better products. Political competition means better candidates, better politics and most importantly, governments that better represent the will of their people.

In my view, the Russian people already understand this. Polls shows that most Russians want to choose their national and local leaders in competitive elections. They want to be able to assemble freely, and they want a media to be independent of the state. And they want to live in a country that fights corruption.

That's democracy. They're the ingredients of democracy. So I urge all of you students here: Don't compromise on the basic elements of democracy. You need not make that Faustian bargain.

And it's also the message I heard recently when President Medvedev said last week -- and I quote him -- "freedom cannot be postponed." Joe Biden didn't say that. The President of Russia said that.

And when Deputy Premier and Finance Minister Kudrin said that "only fair elections can give the authorities the mandate of trust we need to help implement economic reforms." That's a Russian leader, not an American leader.

Russia and America both have a lot to gain if these sentiments are turned into actions, which I am hopeful they will be.

Now, there are some in Russia who say we hold your country to an unreasonably high standard. It is true our expectations are high, but it's because we've learned during the Cold War just how capable the Russian people are. When you launched Sputnik we had to marshal our greatest intellectual talents to begin to meet the challenge. And we had no illusions ever about the capacity of our then-adversary.

And in this new era of partnership, our respect for the Russian people as innovators, as thinkers remains undiminished. Unleashing the intellectual capacity of this country is not only in Russia's interest but it's in America's national interest; and I would argue the world's interest. This is no longer a zero-sum game.

Folks, as you well know, we've already come a long way. I visited Moscow for the first time in '73, but in the summer of '79, I was asked by then President Carter, some 30 years ago, to lead a delegation of United States Senators who were uncertain about the SALT Talks, SALT II -- Strategic Arms Limitation Talks. And I was a strong supporter of that treaty.

But there were a group of new senators who were not familiar with the treaty, and agnostic on it. And I was asked to bring nine of them to Russia. And we sat across -- I sat across a table -- a conference table in the Kremlin, across the table from Leonid Brezhnev. To his left was Defense Minister Ustinov and to his right was Premier Kosygin.

And to state the obvious, it was a very different time. And I recall President Brezhnev was sicker than we thought then. And he excused himself and left the meeting early and turned it over to Kosygin, Premier Kosygin, who in his opening statement said the following -- I will never forget it -- he said: Before we begin our discussion, Senator, let's agree that we do not trust you, and you do not trust us. And we both have good reason. Literally.

He was absolutely right back then. But he would be absolutely wrong today. Russians and Americans inside and outside of government have worked extremely hard to overcome decades of mistrust, to identify common ground, to fashion a more secure and more prosperous future for both countries.

And in the second decade of this new century, the United States and Russia no longer have good reason not to trust one another. There is no good reason not to trust one another.

It's legitimate to be skeptical as you are in dealing with any nation because their self-interest may be different to you. But it's not -- does not translate into: We cannot trust.

If two great nations that for 40 years stood on the opposite sides of the 20th century's deepest divide can stand side-by-side facing the 21st century challenges, it will benefit not just the American people and the Russian people, but all people.

That future is not just the stuff of which dreams are made of. We are already moving in that direction. Yes, it can be knocked off course. But we are already moving in that direction. And I say to you young people in this audience, it's incumbent upon you and incumbent upon the young people of my country to not allow us to get off that path, to stay in this direction.

And I know that for many of you here today, this will be a joint effort -- that you'll join us. There's much to overcome, but there's much we've done. And I would argue that based on what we've recently done, it's a clear indication we can fundamentally change this relationship on a permanent basis.

Thank you all for being so gracious waiting and even more gracious listening. Thank you.

1. How does Vice President Biden describe the Cold War period?

2. Describe the tone of the speech. Do you feel it is critical of Russia or diplomatic?

EXCERPT FROM "REMARKS BY THE VICE PRESIDENT AND GEORGIAN PRIME MINISTER IN A JOINT PRESS CONFERENCE," FROM THE WHITE HOUSE, AUGUST 1, 2017

VICE PRESIDENT PENCE: Prime Minister Kvrikashvili, thank you so much for those words and for the hospitality you have shown me and my family. It was an honor to welcome you to the White House just a few short months ago, and now it's my honor to be welcomed by you to the beautiful and storied nation of Georgia.

The President of the United States of America, President Donald Trump sent me here with a simple message for you and for the people of Georgia: We are with you. We stand with you. We are proud of our friendship and strategic partnership with the nation and the people of Georgia.

In word, I'm here to say America First does not mean America alone. And America stands with Georgia.

This year marks the 25th anniversary of the United States' diplomatic relationship with Georgia, yet this is a nation whose roots stretch back into the mists of history.

Sitting at the crossroads of empires and civilizations -- where East meets West, where North meets South -- Georgia has fostered your own traditions, your own language, and your own identity over the millennia.

Today the people of Georgia are renowned the world over for your vibrant culture, which my wife and I enjoyed last night, at our first Supra dinner, featuring Georgian cuisine and a lot of it, and traditional song and dance from Abkhazia, South Ossetia, and all across Georgia.

We've also been deeply inspired by the rich heritage of faith, and my wife and I look forward to visiting the historic Sioni Cathedral and meeting the Patriarch of the Georgian Orthodox Church this afternoon.

And while this may be my first visit to this nation, the enduring courage and spirit of the Georgian people have long inspired me.

It was only a generation ago that Georgia was still imprisoned inside the then-Soviet Union. When that brutal regime collapsed, you reclaimed your independence and your freedom. You reached out your hand in friendship to Europe and the United States of America -- and we were proud to reach back.

Today, I commended the Prime Minister for Georgia's democratic development, which has brought Georgia closer to unity with Europe and membership in the North Atlantic Treaty Organization. Further progress on the goals that the Prime Minister has set will bring Georgia even closer and NATO even closer to your grasp, and it will strengthen the bond between our nations.

Nowhere is the bond between our two nations stronger than in our shared effort to promote security and stability across the wider world. Georgia is a key strategic partner of the United States of America.

Since 2004, thousands of Georgians have served shoulder-to-shoulder with Americans -- in Kosovo, in Iraq, and in Afghanistan.

In Afghanistan alone, I say with a grateful heart, Georgia has provided more troops on a per-capita basis than any other country in the world. And 31 brave Georgian soldiers have given their lives for the cause of freedom. The American people remember and mourn the sacrifice of your countrymen. They are heroes, all. And they and their families will be enshrined in the hearts of the American people forever.

Later today, I will meet with troops participating in Exercise Noble Partner. This initiative has brought together the armed forces of the United States, Georgia, and many other nations to train together and strengthen Georgia's ability to defend itself, and it's only one of many examples of the United States' commitment to Georgia's security.

President Trump and I stand by the 2008 NATO Bucharest statement, which made it clear that Georgia will one day become a member of NATO.

As I expressed to the Prime Minister, it is heartening to see that Georgia already exceeds NATO's goal of spending 2 percent of its gross domestic product on its national defense. But as we all know, Georgia's investment in defense is an investment borne of necessity.

At this very moment, just 40 miles from where we stand, Russian tanks stand on occupied territory in South Ossetia. Today, Russia continues to occupy one-fifth of Georgian territory.

So to be clear: The United States of America strongly condemns Russia's occupation on Georgia's soil.

The United States supports Georgia's sovereignty and territorial integrity within its internationally recognized borders. And under President Donald Trump, the United States of America will reject any claim, at any time, by any nation that undermines this enduring principle.

President Trump has called on Russia to "cease its destabilizing activities" -- and my purpose here today is to reinforce that message to the people of Georgia.

In a sign of our commitment, very soon, President Trump will sign legislation to strengthen and codify the United States' sanctions against Russia.

As always, our country prefers a constructive relationship with Russia based on cooperation and common interests. But the President and our Congress are unified in our message to Russia: A better relationship, the lifting of sanctions will require Russia to reverse the actions that caused sanctions to be imposed in the first place.

We hope for better days, and we hope for better relations with Russia, but the recent diplomatic action taken by Moscow I can assure will not deter the commitment of the United States to our security, to that of our allies, and to freedom-loving nations around the world like Georgia.

The United States will continue to work with Georgia to reduce your vulnerabilities and counter Russian aggression. And so, too, will we work with Georgia to deepen our ties of commerce of which the Prime Minister just spoke.

The United States has a keen interest in expanding our trade and investment relationship with Georgia, and your ongoing reforms, Mr. Prime Minister, have clearly demonstrated your openness and commitment to a stronger commercial partnership with the West.

Today, I thanked the Prime Minister for his leadership and focus on bringing greater economic opportunity to all of Georgia's citizens.

The Anaklia deep-sea port shows the potential of a stronger bilateral relationship between our nations. American companies are investing alongside their Georgian counterparts in this multi-billion-dollar project. As we look toward the future, our two nations have untold opportunities to contribute even more to each other's prosperity.

The United States has stood with Georgia for a quarter century, and under President Donald Trump, we will continue to stand with you -- as partners, as friends, and one day, we will stand together as allies.

Georgia's future is in the West. And as the people of Georgia have long declared, our strength is now and always will be in our unity.

So thank you, Mr. Prime Minister. Thank you for your hospitality here today. And thank you for the strong leadership that you've provided for this country. We look forward to working with you for the prosperity and the security of the people of Georgia and of our great nation.

Q (As interpreted.) Mr. Vice President, while visiting the Baltic countries, you mentioned that U.S. always stands to guard the safety of the world, that the Americans will always support Georgia's safety. And when we see that the -- on a daily basis, the rights of the people living on the occupied territories are being breached -- what steps may be taken by the Georgian side, alongside with the (inaudible)?

VICE PRESIDENT PENCE: Well, as I said, the United States of America stands strongly for the territorial integrity of Georgia, and we've stood on that principle since the time that Russian tanks overtook Abkhazia and South Ossetia in 2008. And we'll continue to stand strong.
The joint military operations that are taking place today we hope are a visible sign of our commitment to Georgia's sovereignty and to her internationally recognized borders.
We also believe that in addition to security partnership, that a stronger and more prosperous Georgia will lead to a restoration of a whole and free Georgia. And so the United States will continue to look for ways that we can strengthen Georgia not only from the standpoint of its defense and security, but where we can strengthen Georgia economically, creating jobs and opportunity and prosperity, and strengthening the hand of Georgia so that one day, Georgia can once again celebrate its historic territorial integrity intact.

PRIME MINISTER KVRIKASHVILI: (In progress, as inter-preted.) -- so much for your question, and I would like to render my thanks to the Vice President for his clear-cut (inaudible) message, invariable support, which actually we -- which with Georgia (inaudible) our strategic partner in the United States. As it has been noted, our territorial integrity (inaudible) acute problem which requires con-sistent approach on one part to attain in Georgia stability, economic development, and democratic evolvement, as well as (inaudible) in-depth cooperation to achieve the advances in the field of safety.

But the territorial integrity may be resurrected by the peaceful steps, economic development, and by the staunch support of our strategic partners -- first and fore-most, the United States.

Q Mr. Vice President, in light of Russia's retaliation against sanctions, as well as Russia sending 100,000 troops to the eastern end of NATO's territories to drill, do you truly believe the better relationship that you and Pres-ident Trump want with Russia is possible? And if things continue in this direction, could we be headed for another Cold War?

And then, Mr. Prime Minister, you know better than anyone how real the threat of Russia aggression is. The Vice President just said the United States supports Geor-gia's aspirations into NATO. So what concrete assurances do you have that the U.S. will defend you should Russia attack, as President Putin has threatened?

VICE PRESIDENT PENCE: Well, thank you for the ques-tion. President Trump sent me on this journey to send a very clear message to the Baltic States, to the people of

Georgia, and before the end of the day in Montenegro that the United States of America will stand with freedom-loving nations around the world; and that we will do so, as the President has said, not merely with words but with actions.

The presence of American forces in Poland, the presence of the British forces, with whom I met in Estonia at a gathering yesterday, all give material evidence of the commitment of NATO in that region to live up to our Article 5 obligation.

The current Russian exercises, which news reports today suggest will move up to 100,000 Russian troops into Belarus, is simply a confirmation of the importance of clarity within the NATO partnership.

President Trump and I believe that better relations with Russia may be possible. But as the President has said, we'll see.

But negotiations between parties always begin with a recognition and a respect for the position of each party. And with the sanctions that President Trump will sign this week, codifying sanctions that have been in place by the United States, our country is sending a very clear message and calling on our European allies to join us in a very clear message that we mean what we say and say what we mean; that Russia's destabilizing activities in Ukraine, their support for rogue regimes like Iran and Syria and North Korea, that their posture has to change.

But we believe that by being clear and being strong, that we can pursue a dialogue based on mutual understanding. And President Trump holds the view that it's been a lack of clarity and commitment by the United States that's created much of the instability in the world today.

When in the past America had spoken of red lines and not followed through on red lines, many argue that that emboldened others to act in ways that they would not have.

And so President Trump believes that we can have peace through strength. And strong and clear positions, we believe, can create a foundation where authentic dialogue may -- we hope -- result in better relations and in the resolution of long-standing disputes in Ukraine, in Georgia, and in other areas of the world.

PRIME MINISTER KVRIKASHVILI: Thank you, Mr. Vice President, and thank you for the question.

I think the very clear and strong message "we are with you" tells everything. Georgia faces endless provocations daily. On the occupation line, we are facing challenges of borderization, capturing, kidnapping of ethnic Georgians -- violating basic human rights of ethnic Georgians residing on the occupied territories. But the response to that is only even more resolve and consistency and dedication to the goals we set for ourselves.

Integration into NATO is that process which matters for Georgia. Of course, the final goal to join NATO is set by Georgian population, and we are following this very difficult path of reforming Georgia's military system and developing institutional democracy in Georgia.

And believe me, through the consistency and through the dedication, clearness of our messages and unity with our important strategic partners, it will be able for Georgia to reach this very important goal to ensure long-term stability. And it is possible. We Georgians believe that.

Q Mr. Vice President, what are the red lines -- Washington's red lines on Russia, especially in regard to Georgia? And also you said in Estonia that in case of Russia's aggressions against NATO allies, members of the alliance, the United States will intervene. What would be your reaction in case of Russia's aggression against Georgia -- against NATO's partners?

Thank you very much.

And, Mr. Prime Minister, do we have enough patience to wait for NATO membership where we are waiting -- Georgia is waiting for a while? Thank you.

VICE PRESIDENT PENCE: Well, thank you for the question.

The essence of the North Atlantic Treaty Organization is a mutual-defense agreement, that an attack on one is an attack on all. And what the President wanted me to communicate as I travel to our NATO countries, as later today I'll visit the newest members of NATO, is that the United States says what it means and means what it says. And we'll live up to our obligations under Article 5.

With regard to Georgia, we strongly support Georgia's aspiration to become a member of NATO. And we'll continue to work closely with this Prime Minister and the government of Georgia broadly to advance the policies that will facilitate becoming a NATO member. We believe that Georgia has made extraordinary progress -- not just in the past 25 years, but over the last five years, there has been significant progress in Georgia that we believe will strengthen the application for NATO membership.

With regard to the Russian aggression, which took place in 2008, which has as we stand here today Russian tanks parked on Georgian soil 40 miles from where we stand, the United States will continue to be unambiguous in our commitment to the territorial integrity of Georgia.

We will stand for a strong and whole Georgia. We will continue to provide support for the defense and security of Georgia, and we will continue to seek a peaceful resolution that will reestablish the internationally recognized borders of this nation.

PRIME MINISTER KVRIKASHVILI: Thank you, Mr. Vice President. Thank you for question. You said it's about patience. Yet it's about strategic patience I would say. To stay consistent on the road where we are, today we have all practical tools to advance towards NATO membership. We have substantial package. We are implementing it very successfully. We have Georgia Defense Readiness program, jointly with the United States, which is complementary to the substantial package.

And it was said many times by the leaders of our strategic partners -- the United States first, of course, and NATO leadership that no other country has a say to block the membership of Georgia to NATO. It's only NATO members and applicant countries who decide about the future in NATO. And we have made our own decision. Thank you.

Q Thank you. Mr. Vice President, you've talked about the new Russia sanctions bill as an example of U.S. resolve in the face of Russia aggression. But did not the Trump White House oppose this bill, fearing that it relinquishes presidential authority to Congress? What happened in this process that caused the White House to sign on?

And, Mr. Prime Minister, the U.S. intelligence community has concluded that Russia tried to interfere in our presidential election. Living so close to Russia, having dealt with Russian provocations, do you have any advice for the United States in how to cope with Russian efforts to intervene in our elections and influence voters in our country?

VICE PRESIDENT PENCE: Thank you, Peter. Thank you for the question.

President Trump will sign the Russia sanctions bill soon. Our administration had concerns about this legislation when it emerged from the United States Senate. The concern was that it did not include the traditional flexibility that is afforded to the State Department or any administration in the conduct of American foreign policy.

I'm pleased to report that the bill improved significantly as it moved through the House of Representatives and through the legislative process. This legislation we believe will not only codify current Russian sanctions that our administration has upheld, but will also strengthen those sanctions -- even while giving the President of the United States and our State Department the ability and the flexibility to be able to administer American foreign policy as appropriate.

And let me say that in signing the sanction, our President and our Congress are speaking with a unified voice that those matters that the President spoke about so eloquently in Warsaw, about Russian destabilizing activities, about Russia's efforts to support rogue regimes -- that has to change.

For there to be a change in our relationship with Russia, Russia has to change its behavior. And by these sanctions, by my presence here, by the President's powerful affirmation of the objectives and the values of our alliance in the West, our hope is that we will move toward better relations and a better future and a more peaceful world as a result.

PRIME MINISTER KVRIKASHVILI: Thank you. First of all, let me once again mention how important is strong America for Georgia. We are genuinely interested in the strength of the United States, and we would like to see the United States united to cope with the global challenges.

I don't think that Georgia is in a position to judge about Russian interference. With our excellent intelligence capabilities, we were not able to detect any interference, and we think that American nation has made its decision to elect a President. And of course, we look for more partnership with the current administration of the United States."

1. Explain the connection between Russia and Georgia, and how it relates to the "new Cold War."

2. Compare and contrast this speech with the one given by Vice President Biden. Do you feel the two speeches are very different or similar in tone?

"MCCAIN WARNS AGAINST RUSSIAN OVERTURES, A DAY AFTER TRUMP, PUTIN TALK," BY ALLIE BICE, FROM *CRONKITE NEWS*, NOVEMBER 15, 2016

WASHINGTON – Sen. John McCain, R-Arizona, issued a stern warning Tuesday against smoothing relations with Russia, one day after President-elect Donald Trump and Russian President Vladimir Putin agreed that the two countries need to do just that.

McCain did not mention Trump by name in a statement released by his office, noting only Putin's overtures "with the U.S. presidential transition underway." But he warned that another "reset" of relations would make the U.S. complicit in Russia's "butchery of the Syrian people," among other crimes.

"When America has been at its greatest, it is when we have stood on the side those fighting tyranny," said the statement from McCain, who is chairman of the Senate Armed Services Committee. "That is where we must stand again."

The statement came on the heels of a Russian statement outlining a Monday phone call in which Putin congratulated Trump and said he wanted to begin a partnership based on "equality, mutual respect and non-interference in each other's domestic affairs."

It went on to say the two men "agreed on the absolutely unsatisfactory state of bilateral relations" and the need to improve them.

An adviser to the Trump transition team, Army Lt. Gen. Joseph Keith Kellogg, defended discussions with

Russia about improved relations. While Kellogg said he was not speaking for the transition team, he said "it's an appropriate way that world leaders talk. So I think it's great."

"They're a global nuclear power and you need to have good relations with them," Kellogg said, according to a press pool report from Trump Tower in New York.

Trump said several times during the campaign that he admired Putin for his strong leadership – sparking an outcry from critics who noted Russian incursions in Ukraine, Georgia and Syria, and oppression of domestic groups.

McCain isn't the only senator with deep reservations about a "reset" on relations with Russia. Sen. Lindsey Graham, R-South Carolina, called this "a defining moment for the country."

"I want a good relationship with Russia, but things have to substantially change," said Graham, an ally of McCain's and the chairman of a Senate Appropriations subcommittee on foreign operations.

Graham, who mounted an unsuccessful run for the GOP presidential nomination this year, said it is up to Trump as commander-in-chief to establish better relations with Russia, but added that "Congress has a role in all this."

"He is the leading diplomat to the country, but Congress has a role," he said.

"When it comes to all things Russia, I am going to be kind of hard-ass," Graham said, calling for a series of hearings "about Russia's misadventures throughout the world."

McCain said the U.S. should continue to question Putin's intentions given his history.

"We should place as much faith in such statements as any other made by a former KGB agent who has plunged his country into tyranny, murdered his political opponents, invaded his neighbors, threatened America's allies, and attempted to undermine America's elections," McCain's statement said.

1. Why do Senators McCain and Graham voice concern over relations with Russia?

2. Do you agree that relations with Russia should be conducted carefully, or should the United States work harder to bridge the diplomatic gap?

CHAPTER 3

WHAT SOCIAL MEDIA EXPERTS SAY

Soft power was at the core of the Cold War, serving as a way for both the United States and the Soviet Union to grow their spheres of influence through culture and propaganda. Today, social media is serving as the battleground between Russia and the United States; the role of social media in connecting the world is also making it a primary tool for countries to spread their message and undermine their rivals. This was made clear in 2016, when Russia used targeted ads on Facebook and Twitter accounts to spread disinformation. At the same time, China has been shaping the way social media can be used in their country, effectively controlling the flow of information into and out of the country. Social media experts have been closely observing the way these countries use social media and what it could mean for the Cold War in a new era.

98

"FAKE NEWS AND FAKE SOLUTIONS: HOW DO WE BUILD A CIVICS OF TRUST?," BY IVAN SIGAL, FROM *GLOBAL VOICES*, MARCH 20, 2017

In his recent manifesto, Mark Zuckerberg asserts that the response to our dysfunctional and conflict-ridden politics is to build a stronger global community based on ubiquitous interconnection. We know of course that Facebook stands to profit from this utopian vision, and we should be skeptical of the motives underlying Zuck's position. But it's worth taking a second look at the idea of working on underlying economic and political issues in our societies, rather than focusing on the effects of online expression—particularly in the context of the moral panic over "fake news."

The consternation about fake news from Western journalists, scholars of propaganda, and policymakers has inspired waves of stories and talk-shops addressing its growth as a threat to our public discourse, our journalism, and our systems of governance. And we see many attempts to understand, fix, or apportion blame. Yet many of the proposed fixes are deeply problematic because they advocate overly broad and vague restrictions on expression. Solutions that would limit suspected "fake" expression or strongly encourage private intermediaries to restrict some kinds of speech and prioritize or "whitelist" others are particularly troubling.

This week, Germany was the latest country to introduce a plan that would force social media companies to monitor and censor some kinds of online expression. Justice minister Heiko Maas wants to put regulatory pressure on social media companies, and especially Facebook and Twitter, to police expression, asserting that they have failed to do so voluntarily. Draft legislation proposes to fine social media companies up to 50 million for failure to quickly delete hate speech, fake news, and other types of misleading speech.

In this context, we can look to countries that have created regulatory regimes to control online expression — such as China — not as entirely "other", but perhaps as cautionary examples. When posing solutions to fix fake news, we should be extremely careful not to build our own self-censorship machines.

"FAKE" NEWS AND THE ROLE OF STATES

Many recent false news stories have come from groups not affiliated with states, but examples from Russia, China, Iran and many other countries should remind us that the biggest threat to our public discourse is false information used by and to the advantage of governments. Governments, after all, have the authority to couple shifting narratives of truth to state mechanisms of control. We ought to be especially attuned to states that restrict the "false" expression of their citizens, while at the same time creating misleading narratives and stories about themselves. When states attempt to control narratives, it's time to start looking for signs of tyranny.

For the past 20 years, we have seen states or their affiliates use Internet-based false news and disinformation as part of broader agendas to shape public opinion for political ends. Well-researched examples include China's 50 Cent Party, Russia's troll factories, and astroturfing bot engines contracted by the U.S. government, all of which are designed to flood Internet forums and social media with falsities and distractions.

At the same time, some states have taken steps to regulate, restrict and even criminalize "false" stories produced by citizens and journalists as a punitive method of controlling expression. In Bahrain, China, Egypt, Turkey, Russia, Venezuela, Iran and elsewhere social media users have been arrested and prosecuted for sharing information deemed by governments to be false or misinformed. New regulations in China forbid the use of "unverified facts distributed via social media platforms" and prohibit websites "from quoting from unnamed or fake news sources and fabricating news based on hearsay, guesswork or imagination."

A recent declaration issued by a group of intergovernmental organizations, including UN Rapporteur for Freedom of Expression David Kaye, discusses these regulatory efforts from the perspective of international law and norms. They emphasize that international human rights doctrine explicitly protects expression that may differ from or counter governmental positions, even when it is factually inaccurate. Regulatory and technical approaches to reduce fake news should, they argue, continue to safeguard the diversity and abundance of speech. They write:

> the human right to impart information and ideas is not limited to "correct" statements…the right also protects information and ideas that may shock, offend and disturb, and that prohibitions on disinformation may violate international human rights standards, while, at the same time, this does not justify the dissemination of knowingly or recklessly false statements by official or State actors…

WHAT'S THE PROBLEM, EXACTLY?

The real-life consequences of fake news are unclear. A recent study by the MIT/Harvard research project Media Cloud, (with which Global Voices is affiliated), led by Yochai Benkler and Ethan Zuckerman, examines the effects of right-wing information sources in the U.S. It suggests that rather than wringing our hands over "fake news", we should focus on disinformation networks that are insulated from mainstream public conversations. Benkler and his colleagues challenge the idea that "the internet as a technology is what fragments public discourse and polarizes opinions" and instead argue that "human choices and political campaigning, not one company's algorithm" are the more likely factor to influence the construction and dissemination of disinformation.

Nevertheless, projects seeking to control fake news are running full steam ahead. These efforts have the potential to affect what information is easily available to publics, and if we aren't careful, could even diminish our rights to expression. Approaches tend to fall into three broad categories:

- Fix online discourse by nudging technologies that control or censor some categories of speech
- Fix the public by making us better at distinguishing fact from fallacy
- Fix journalism, generally with massive cash transfers from the technology sector

Notably, these approaches all focus on mitigating effects rather than confronting the underlying economic or technical incentives in the structure of media, or the broader social, economic and political incentives that motivate speech.

FIX ONLINE DISCOURSE

In seeking to build systems to manage false news, technology companies will end up creating systems to monitor and police speech. We will quickly find that they need to use ever-more granular, vigilant and therefore continuously updated semantic analysis in order to find and restrict expression.

These proposed solutions to fake news would be in part technological, based on AI and natural language processing. They will automate the search for and flagging of certain terms, word associations, and linguistic formulations. But language is more malleable than algorithm, and we will find that people will invent alternative terms and locutions to express their ends.

The slipperiness of language could cause the hunt for "fake" or hurtful speech to become an end in itself. We have already seen this in the hunt for "toxic" language in a recent project called Perspective, made by Google's Jigsaw, and other efforts will surely follow.

Companies are likely to supplement their automated processes with human monitoring — from social media platform users flagging suspect content to contractor armies interpreting those flags and implementing restrictions. Added to this, perhaps, will be ombudspeople, feedback loops, legal processes, and policy controls upon the censors. Those systems are already in place to deal with terrorism, extreme hate speech, extreme violence, child pornography, and nudity and sexual arousal. They can be further refined and expanded to police other types of expression.

Proposed solutions in this vein mostly fail to acknowledge that the technological incentives that encourage fake news are the same as the forces that currently finance the digital media industry — that is, advertising technology masquerading as editorial content.

The internet theorist Doc Searls calls this "adtech", emphasizing that it is a form of direct marketing or spamming. The rise of fake news is driven in part by organizations seeking revenues or political influence by creating sensational and misleading stories packaged for highly polarized audiences. Producers of this content benefit from a system already designed to segment and mobilize audiences for commercial ends. That system includes the monitoring of consumer habits, targeted advertising, direct marketing and the creation of editorial products appealing to specific consumer segments. These forces coalesce in a dance of editorial and advertising incentives that leads to further polarization and segmentation.

FIX THE PUBLIC

The next approach — that we fix ourselves — relies on the Victorian idea that our media systems would work if only people behaved in ways expected of them by the builders of systems. Media literacy campaigns, public education, fact-checking, calling out and shaming tactics, media diets, whitelists of approved media: these solutions require that we blame ourselves for failing to curb our appetites. It is not wrong to suggest that we are susceptible to the allure of the media's endorphin-injection strategy to hook us on the sensational and trivial, or that education is important for a healthy civics. To focus blame primarily on individuals, however, is victim-blaming of a sort.

FIX JOURNALISM

The third approach — devoting more resources to better journalism, is an example of the journalism community jumping on the current moment to reassert their expertise and value. While a more proactive, better-resourced media is definitely vital for the long-term health of our civic life, conversations about journalism need to start with the trust deficit many journalistic outfits have accumulated over the past decades. That deficit exists precisely because of ever-more sensational and facile reporting, news as entertainment, and the corporate drive to maximise profits over the interests of audiences and readers.

Given that the business model of the liberal, capitalist media is primarily to sell eyeballs to advertisers, they should not be surprised to find those of us being sold becoming wise to the approach. And while efforts to strengthen journalism and public trust in the media are important and much-needed, they will not make fake news go away.

SO WHAT ARE WE REALLY TALKING ABOUT?

The technological and the human-based approaches to controlling inaccurate online speech proposed to date for the most part do not address the underlying social, political or communal causes of hateful or false expression. Instead, they seek to restrict behaviors and control effects, and they rely on the good offices of our technology intermediaries for that service. They do not ask us to look more closely at the social and political construction of our communities.

They do not examine and propose solutions to address hate, discrimination and bias in our societies, in issues such as income disparity, urban planning, educational opportunity, or, in fact, our structures of governance.

Frustratingly, we have seen these approaches before, in efforts to reduce online "extremism", and also with dubious results. Countering violent extremism (CVE) projects suffer from similar definitional flaws about the nature of the problem, but that doesn't stop governments from creating misguided responses. For examples, look to the many 'counter-narrative' projects such as "Welcome to ISIS Land" funded by the U.S. State Department. These projects, supported by governments, international organizations, and companies, seek an array of technical, communications and policy-based approaches to controlling extremism.

David Kaye, in an earlier joint declaration on CVE, notes the "fail[ure] to provide definitions for key terms, such as 'extremism' or 'radicalization'. "In the absence of a clear definition, these terms can be used to restrict a wide range of lawful expression," but still inflict collateral damage, with pervasive surveillance and tracking that triggers the self-censor in all of us, resulting in the reduction of civic participation and dialogue.

How do we begin to tackle the larger challenges, those beyond simple technological fixes or self-blame? There are no easy solutions for the economic and social inequities that create divisions, and the technological and economic incentives that underpin our current information ecosystem are deeply entrenched. Yet we need to find a way to start serious conversations about these systemic challenges, rather than tinkering with their effects or simply assigning responsibility to the newest players on the field.

Sir Tim Berners-Lee, the inventor of the internet, has urged that we reform the systems and business models we have created to fund our online lives. He points, for example, to the use of personal data by companies as the driver for the creation of surveillance societies, which exerts chilling effects on free expression. He suggests seeking alternatives to the concentration of attention and power in the hands of a small number of social media companies that derive profit from showing us content that is "surprising, shocking, or designed to appeal to our biases." He's concerned by the use of these same tactics in political advertising, and its effect on our systems of electoral politics.

Confronting our social and economic inequities is even harder. It is the challenge of our time to find the language to conduct honest and frank debate about how we construct our economies and our states, how we apportion benefits, and which values guide us. Building civic communities that are rooted in trust, both online and off, is the ongoing and vital work necessary for public conversations about our collective future.

It is no small irony that the communications systems that we built to support such debate are imperilled, both by those who would explode the social norms of civic discourse for their ideological ends, and through resultant attempts to control extreme or misleading expression. It is easy to find fault with the technologies that facilitate our collective civic life. It is much more difficult to look at our civic life as a whole and determine whether and how it may be failing.

1. What role does trust play in social media according to the author?

2. What needs to be done to undermine attempts at using social media to disrupt civic society?

"FACEBOOK'S 'FAKE NEWS' PLAN IS DOOMED TO FAILURE – SOCIAL MEDIA MUST DO MORE TO COUNTER DISINFORMATION," BY TOM FELLE, FROM *THE CONVERSATION*, APRIL 11, 2017

Fake news has become an important focus for news foundations, democratic interest groups and various journalism academics and researchers, following claims that the US presidential elections may have been influenced by anti-Clinton propaganda created by Russia and shared on social networks.

In recent weeks there has been a concerted effort by news organisations and social networks to combat the proliferation of so-called "fake news" online.

Facebook recently announced a three-day campaign to warn users in 14 countries about sharing content without knowing its origin. The notice: "Tips to Spot False News" advised users to be wary of headlines, to look closely at URLs and investigate the source of material before sharing it.

However Adam Mosseri, Facebook's vice president of news feed, said there was "no silver bullet" to solve the problem.

The German government has proposed fining social media platformsand other digital publishers up to €50m if they fail to promptly remove fake news, hate speech and other illegal content.

Google also recently updated a limited fact-checking tag to alert users about search results in its feed. Meanwhile the threat of far-right extremists trying to hijack the French election via social networks is being taken very seriously by media companies and social networks in France, who are working together to fact check news.

SEVEN DEGREES OF FAKERY

But the problem with fake news is that the term has become a euphemism for everything from satire, to information shared out of context, to malicious content created with the intention of deceiving and potentially influencing public opinion.

It is even used by some – including the US president, Donald Trump – to describe news we just don't like or disagree with.

Clare Wardle at First Draft News has created a "misinformation matrix" of seven types of mis and disin-formation, ranking stories from poor journalism to content produced for profit, political influence or propaganda.

Some of the "fake" news shared on social networks is funny. But worryingly, there is a suspicion, even alle-gations, that malicious false news has been, and is being, created to "game" social media and search algo-rithms and influence public opinion, as is alleged to have happenedin the run up to the US presidential elections.

News companies must bear some blame for being duped into believing their future success lay at the end of a social media rainbow. News companies desperate to survive have been consumed with metrics, producing increasingly generic content optimised for social sharing to reach ever greater audiences. But in doing so they have lost a vital connection with their audience. On social media, users are promiscuous and no longer connect the news they consume and share with the news companies that produced it in the first place.

Social networks and other algorithm-based aggregators had turned a blind eye to the problem, their algorithms rewarding "content" that drives engagement, rather than ranking on trust and truth. Investigations by Buzzfeed's media editor Craig Silverman found that fake news companies were making significant revenue from traffic generated as a result of shares on social platforms and other aggregators.

More worryingly, though, the same "gaming" of the algorithms may be used for propaganda or to influence public opinion. And there lies the real threat of fake news. In a post-truth society, trust in institutions including the media has reached its nadir. But we trust our friends and families – and we trust what they share on social media, and are more influenced by it.

Whatever their editorial leaning, traditional news organisations – and the journalists that staffed them – had an overriding public interest function. Tech companies have no such lofty ideals. Even if Facebook itself would never attempt to influence public opinion via its timeline, the very fact that news that appears in timelines is based on algorithms is already a cause for concern, because algorithms can be gamed.

ALGORITHMS RULE, OK?

Now that they have been publicly embarrassed into taking action, the next step for tech companies and social networks in combating fake news will be based on algorithms pre-filtering content, rather than any overriding public interest or editorial decision making. But what if the *Guardian* runs an expose on a major shareholder in Facebook or *The New York Times* uncovers uncomfortable truths about a past or future relationship between a major social network and national security services? How will social media algorithms deal with stories like that? In an era where news is increasingly viewed via social networks, these networks are the new gatekeepers – and they hold all the keys.

If the public only ever gets to see content that has been pre-filtered, this will have serious implications for free speech and quality journalism – especially journalism that argues against prevailing viewpoints. Social networks will disintegrate into echo chambers where dissenting voices are drowned out in favour of news and opinion that chimes with a pre-filtered view based on the algorithm's data about an individual user's views of preferences.

No news organisation has ever commanded as much power to shape public opinion as Facebook – and yet its founder Mark Zuckerberg clings steadfastly to the mantra that the social network is not a media company, and so has no editorial function.

Digital literacy is part of the answer and Facebook's latest foray was in part an attempt to alert audiences to be more sceptical about what they see and what they share. But in doing so, Facebook is abdicating its own responsibility to address the problem head on.

Zuckerberg's claims are wearing thin. Until Facebook faces up to the reality that it has an editorial responsibility to its audience and to news organisations that help produce quality, trusted news, the problem will never be solved.

1. What does the author mean by "fake news" and why does it need to be addressed?

2. What is Facebook doing to combat "fake news"? Does the author feel this is enough?

"UKRAINE, KREMLIN PROPAGANDA AND THE COLD WAR TRAP," BY AMMON CHESKIN, FROM *THE CONVERSATION*, MARCH 25, 2014

Facebook can be a confusing place. For the follower of Ukrainian and Russian politics the messages could not be more different. At the same time that "Euromaidan PR" is posting pictures of "Putler" and accusing Russia of being a sick, backwards imperial bully, "Voice of Russia" is relaying to the world how Ukraine is overrun by fascists, bankrolled by the US and the EU, and at the point of political and economic ruin.

I used to be of the opinion that propaganda was more sophisticated in 2014 than in 1944. The current media war appears to tell a different story.

To get a sense of the levels of absurdity the propaganda has reached, one need look no further than the Voice of Russia, a Kremlin-sponsored, international media outlet that claims to have 109m listeners worldwide. International it might be, but objective it certainly is not. Voice of Russie is an integral part of Moscow's concerted campaign to increase its "soft power" abroad. Linked with other international media, cultural foundations, and business organisations, Voice of Russia aims to promote a more positive image of Russia to the world, and to move beyond Cold War stereotypes.

However, such stereotypes have become a recent staple for Russian media outlets that have been increasingly subservient to Vladimir Putin's ever-more authoritarian regime. In recent days three overarching themes dominate Voice of Russia reporting. First, the West (especially America) is evil, duplicitous, greedy, and arrogant. Second, Russia (especially Putin) is strong, righteous, and morally superior to the west.

Third, these two main stances are justified by asserting vigorously that Ukraine is overrun by anarchic fascists, anti-Semites, and haters of everything Russian. The fact that the West has supported these "fascists", while Russia is gallantly trying to protect Russians and Russian-speakers, is cited as concrete proof that the West is indeed morally bankrupt, but Russia is acting entirely honourably.

FRIENDS REUNITED

But don't take my word for it. Here are some of the headlines from Voice of Russia's Facebook feed from the past week: "Fascism seeps into America amid Ukraine crisis", "Putin's rating has hit a five-year high", "Obama's presidency ... has been a force of pure evil",

"Crimea re-joins Russia after US/Nazi coup in Ukraine". The list could go on. Most commonly, Voice of Russia hands over space to dubious western "experts" with extreme views who are happy to berate the United States of America and who presumably know very little about Ukraine and the events in Kiev or Crimea.

Of course there is little point discussing the journalistic or moral credibility of Voice of Russia, or the various other domestic and international media sources that are similarly being filled with such blatant propaganda. Many, such as Stopfake.org, are rigorously attempting to counter Russian propaganda by exposing the inconsistencies, biases, and factual inaccuracies of the media coverage. Nevertheless, while most commentators can see this propaganda for what it is, it still has a number of grave consequences.

These messages appear to be going down rather well in Russia. The cynic might note that Russian media and the Kremlin have been gearing up for this heightened propaganda war well in advance of the Ukraine crisis. In recent years the authorities have steadily been ratcheting up their anti-western rhetoric, promoting instead traditional "Russian values" of heterosexuality, sovereign democracy, and Orthodoxy. This has been a useful means to ensure domestic support.

A pressing question is how to deal with this media onslaught. Fight fire with fire perhaps as a number of Ukrainian social media groups are attempting to do? The problem with this is that we can fall into the same trap of overt subjectivity. A group of respected academics and experts on Ukraine signed an online petition asking western media sources to stop focusing exclusively on the role of the far-right in the Maidan protests, arguing that this plays into the hands of the Kremlin.

This demonstrates the power of Russia's propaganda. It forces many to adopt a fully subjective and partisan position. Knowing that the Kremlin's well-oiled propaganda machine will instantly seize upon any negative reporting or commentary of the role of the far-right in Ukraine, shouldn't we just focus on the democratic majority that characterised the Maidan movement?

But this retreat into subjectivity would signal a major victory for Putin's efficient media structures. Russia's incessant propaganda is devalued because it lacks credibility. Scholarly and journalistic scrutiny of Russia must be accompanied by open debate, self-criticism, and honest reflection. These democratic principles are intolerable in a functioning authoritarian regime.

We should therefore admit that: yes, the USA and other European countries have often acted poorly on the international stage; yes, the IMF can be a disruptive and deeply problematic entity; yes the EU did not sufficiently take into account Russian interests and concerns in Ukraine; and yes, there are many aspects of Ukraine's domestic politics that are deeply troubling.

By admitting and debating these issues we will be able to state with moral authority that: no, Ukraine is not overrun by fascists; no, Russia is not acting in the best interests of its compatriots; no, it is not acceptable to violate the territorial integrity of another country; and no, the Crimean referendum was in no way constitutional, moral, or democratic.

"WHAT'S FUELING CHINA'S AGGRESSIVE CRACKDOWN ON ACTIVISM AND MEDIA?," BY MATT MOIR, FROM *WAGING NON-VIOLENCE*, MAY 12, 2016

Ilshat Hassan is a person not easily frightened.

Chinese security forces have detained Hassan, an ethnic Uyghur from China's troubled Xinjiang province, on multiple occasions. He's been beaten in police custody and shocked with an electric cattle prod.

In a particularly harrowing incident, he's even had an assault rifle pointed at him by an agitated paramilitary officer.

It was 1998, and Hassan was on a long-distance bus trip to visit his parents' home in Xinjiang. In the middle of the night, during a particularly isolated stretch of the journey, the bus was stopped and boarded by armed security officials.

All of the Uyghurs on board were ordered off the bus to the side of the road. After a tense standoff, he and his group were able to continue along their way. Still, the incident rattled him.

"It was a difficult experience," he recalled. "Because I'm Uyghur, I'm nothing to them. I'm nothing to

[China], nothing to that system. They can throw me in the trash at any time, at any moment."

Although Hassan was shaken by the incident, he continued to agitate for the rights of his fellow Uyghurs, China's beleaguered ethnic and religious minority. But today, nearly two decades later and living comfortably near Washington, D.C. — where he serves as the interim president of the Uyghur American Association — Hassan is more unsettled than ever by the Chinese authorities.

An article that he recently wrote for a Mandarin-language website caught the eye of officials in Beijing. The piece was critical of the Chinese government, and in retaliation security officers arrested and detained Hassan's sister in Xinjiang.

She was eventually released, but — not surprisingly — Hassan is still concerned for his family's safety should he again write something that runs afoul of China's censors.

Considering the current political and human rights landscape in China, Hassan — and many others — might have good reason to worry.

A FEROCITY NOT SEEN IN YEARS

Since coming to power in 2012, the Xi Jingping government has treated China's 1.3 billion citizens to a grim buffet of unabashed authoritarianism. Security officials have limited Internet freedom, shut down magazines and websites, closely monitored social media, spied on university students and instructors, harassed religious worshippers, and — of course — arrested and detained hundreds of human rights lawyers and activists.

The Chinese Communist Party's robust efforts to check freedom of expression and personal liberties have not been conducted in secret. In fact, the United States, along with 11 other nations, recently issued a statement at the United Nations Human Rights Council criticizing China's rights record. Also, Human Rights Watch's 2015 World Report notes that Chinese "authorities have unleashed an extraordinary assault on basic human rights and their defenders with a ferocity unseen in years."

Nevertheless, the situation over the last several months has only deteriorated.

In January, the Chinese authorities shut down a prominent women's legal aid clinic in the capital. Beijing Zhongze Women's Legal Counseling and Service Center, a symbol of civil society progressivism for two decades, was shuttered indefinitely without explanation.

A high-profile Protestant leader, Rev. Gu Yuese, was arrested in February, the latest move in a campaign to limit the rapid growth of Christianity in China. The clergyman was the most senior government-sanctioned church leader to be arrested since the Cultural Revolution.

Lawyers continue to figure prominently in Beijing's repression of dissidents. In April, a human rights lawyer was arrested after he reposted material linking President Xi to the Panama Papers, and another had his license revoked after criticizing the government on social media.

The Communist Party's authoritarian grasp has also shown an increased willingness to reach across the South China Sea. In a case that made headlines all over the world, five Hong Kong booksellers who worked at a publishing house and bookstore that sold materials critical of the Communist Party were arrested on the Chinese mainland earlier this year under mysterious circumstances. Two of the booksellers have been released, but three are still in police custody.

Indeed, there are almost daily reports of activists being harassed and detained for their work. Much of the coverage of those cases, however, comes from foreign media outlets. That's because news media run by the Communist Party must, according to President Xi, strictly follow the party leadership and focus on "positive reporting."

Speaking at a media symposium in February, Xi said that "all news media run by the party must work to speak for the party's will and its propositions and protect the party's authority and unity."

Xi also added that journalists "should enhance their awareness to align their ideology, political thinking and deeds to those of the CPC Central Committee and help fashion the party's theories and policies into conscious action by the general public while providing spiritual enrichment to the people."

"In a country where media is highly controlled by government, there is limited space for media development," said a Chinese news editor at a larger international media organization, who does not want his name published. "Self-censorship exists in almost every Chinese local media [outlet]. Chinese media workers will have very different ideas on censorship than those working for foreign media."

ECONOMIC ANXIETY

Experts fear the crackdown on activism and media point to a broadening Communist Party attack on what it considers potential threats to its authority.

"The detentions are especially disturbing when we recall that Xi Jinping himself talked about the importance of the rule of law on more than one occasion after he became the leader of China's party-state," said Josephine Chui-Duke, professor of Chinese intellectual history at the University of British Columbia in Vancouver. "China's political decisions and practices are usually never transparent to the outside world, but one thing that seems quite clear is that the recent intensification of their repressive measures must have something to do with their fear of losing control over these rights movements in Chinese society."

Other China watchers attribute aggressive moves against civil society to a government made jittery by an underperforming economy: The country's GDP grew by just 6.9 percent in 2015, the weakest annual growth rate in 25 years.

"The faltering economy has put pressure on the party to try and strengthen its own hold on power because its prestige has been degraded by the fact that it's not able to deliver the economic benefits that it has in the years following the Cultural Revolution until fairly recently," said Charles Burton, associate professor of Chinese politics at Brock University in St. Catharines, Ontario, and former diplomat at the Canadian embassy in Beijing.

Anxiety over the future performance of the Chinese economy might explain why authorities are particularly sensitive to the criticisms of grassroots campaigns, whether those campaigns are environmentalist, religious or political in nature.

In other words, if activists feel emboldened to criticize the lack of personal freedoms afforded to the Chinese people, they might also feel brazen enough to take on the party's handling of the economy. For a government whose legitimacy rests upon the improvement of living conditions and increase of material success of the people, this is unacceptable.

"The party plans to carry out a systematic suppression of civil society until all the dissident voices and alternative narratives about Chinese politics and history and culture are silenced," Burton said. "The question is: Are the people in China prepared to accept a regime that is so much at odds with the value of ordinary people, particularly urban, middle-class people?"

Zhiqun Zhu, an expert in contemporary Chinese politics, suggests that they are. He believes that many Chinese people don't have a problem with Xi's creeping cult of personality, as long as the president continues to root out corruption.

"With so many thorny problems to deal with, such as rampant corruption, you need a strong — a very strong — leader at the top. This explains why Xi remains popular at the grassroots level despite all the problems perceived by Western observers. This has a lot to do with China's paternalistic culture," said Zhiqun Zhu, associate professor of political science and international relations and director of the China Institute at Bucknell University in Lewisburg, Pennsylvania.

According to Zhu, the average Chinese person prioritizes the pursuit of a better material life over protesting anti-democratic activity. The reality in today's China is that liberal voices among the Communist Party have been effectively neutralized, and there just aren't any viable alternatives to the current regime's hardline approach. And even if there were, many might reject it anyway.

"In the end," Zhu explained, "[the Chinese people] tend to agree with the party that maintaining stability is preferable to any sort of 'color revolution,' which may lead to instability and chaos."

BRAINWASHING THE CHINESE PEOPLE

Meanwhile, Ilshat Hassan, the Uyghur activist mistreated by the Chinese government, doesn't hold any grudges against the Chinese people. After being granted political asylum in Malaysia, he came into contact with many ethnic Chinese from Malaysia, Indonesia and Taiwan. Hassan describes the Chinese Muslims, Christians and Buddhists he met as "very traditional, very kind people."

He has no such views on the current Chinese regime, however.

"The root [problem] is the Communist dictatorship," he said. "It brainwashed the Chinese people. They became indifferent to the violation of their neighbor's rights."

Nor does he believe the country of his birth is moving in the right direction.

"Every day, there are new outrages. For journalists, lawyers, activists these are very dangerous times. Even for regular people."

1. What justification is China providing for cracking down on activists and journalists?

2. What can this kind of restriction on information and media tell us about China's place in a Cold War dynamic?

"RUSSIA'S AGGRESSIVE POWER IS RESURGENT, ONLINE AND OFF," BY FRANK J. CILLUFFO, FROM *THE CONVERSATION*, AUGUST 26, 2016

The Bear is back. It's happening on the ground in and around Ukraine, inside the virtual inboxes of the Democratic National Committee and at American news organizations. Russian cyberattacks are yielding eye-popping headlines warning not only of a return to Cold War-style behavior, but of the relative decline of American capabilities and power.

The list of U.S. entities believed to have been breached by Russian hackers is long and troubling. It includes the White House, the State Department, the Defense Department, the NASDAQ stock exchange, the U.S. electrical grid and the Democratic National Committee. Russian cyberattackers have also attempted to hack the Moscow bureau of *The New York Times.*

As the targets have moved beyond U.S. government to key civilian institutions, there has been a good deal of speculation about possible motives. These range from a desire to influence the outcome of November's U.S. presidential election to the broader goal of undermining U.S.-European relations.

What do we know about Russia's capabilities, strategies and intents? And what should we know about this top-notch adversary, more advanced and stealthier than any other, so we can most effectively assess and address the prospect of a Russian threat?

A DEFT AND POWERFUL PLAYER

The United States remains a powerhouse of innovation and technological capacity. But the country is not alone when it comes to sophisticated tools and tradecraft in the cyber domain. Key players comprising Russia's "cyber arsenal" include Russia's foreign intelligence service (SVR), military intelligence agency (GRU), Federal Security Service (FSB), and Federal Protective Service (FSO).

Testifying before the U.S. Senate Armed Services Committee earlier this year, U.S. Director of National Intelligence James Clapper noted that Russia's cyberattacks are becoming more brazen, "based on its willingness to target critical infrastructure systems and conduct espionage operations even when detected and under increased public scrutiny."

Since the fall of the Berlin Wall, Russia's security and intelligence services have practiced the world's second-oldest profession using high-tech tactics. Years ago, Russia was quick to recognize and integrate the potential leverage that online tools and action could offer to military doctrine, strategy and operations. But recently Russia has been honing this model of war fighting, blending electronic and real-world power into a hybrid that is more than the sum of its parts.

The first lessons came from Russia's 2008 conflict with neighboring Georgia. By 2013, Valery Gerasimov, chief of the General Staff of the Armed Forces of the Russian Federation, was laying out the Russian military doctrine for the 21st century with emphasis on "nonmilitary means" (such as political and economic actions) supported by "concealed" military efforts (such as activities undertaken by special operations troops – or cyberspace operatives). Starting in 2014, that integrated approach was used in battle with Ukraine.

Attacks directed against the United States and other countries' governments and businesses have yielded economic and diplomatic secrets that serve to strengthen Russia's industries and negotiating hand in matters of trade and global politics. Put bluntly, stealing the results of others' research is faster and cheaper than investing oneself, just as knowing other players' cards makes deciding a poker player's next moves easier and more effective.

CONCEALING ITS TRUE MOTIVES

Russia makes extensive use of surrogates to further the country's objectives. These groups and individuals may be directly supported and sanctioned by the Russian state, or they may simply be operating at a level of remove that affords Russian officials plausible deniability. This in itself is not new: Russia has long relied on proxies to conceal its own hand and engage in deception – a practice known as "maskirovka." In the digital context, accurately identifying who is behind the keyboard is an ongoing challenge even for the most tech-savvy among us, though the U.S. and other countries are getting better at it.

Beyond identity, intentions are always tricky to establish correctly from the outside. Recall, for example, the Cold War practice of Kremlinology–analyzing the Soviet Union's government and policies to determine its future actions – which fell short of science even at the best of times. Some cases, however, are easier to analyze than others. For instance, Russian cybercriminals are assuredly motivated by the prospect of profits. But the lines between criminals and state-backed attackers are not necessarily well-defined; there have been reports about the convergence between the two groups in Russia – with this confluence serving to magnify the country's cyber capacity.

There are many reasons these manifestations of Russian capability and threat matter: They can destabilize countries and regions, and bring economic or even physical harm directly or indirectly to U.S. interests and those of our allies. These types of damage are real, if not always fully tangible.

Determined Russian propagandizing online has advanced narratives that seek to undercut "the institutions of the West" and spread social unrest in target countries. One method has been spreading fear of immigrants. In January 2016, Russian media outlets carried a fake story alleging a Russian girl had been raped in Berlin by a refugee.

Increasing our knowledge of Russia's capabilities, motives and intentions will allow us not only to deter attacks and respond to ones that happen, but also to act in ways that influence Russia's behavior toward outcomes the U.S. deems desirable. Today's digital threats are at once pervasive and profound, with no single defense or solution. We need more research into potential countermeasures tailored to specific adversaries if we are to thwart them and bolster U.S. national and economic security.

1. Explain the relationship between Russia's tactics online and offline.

2. Based on the author's arguments, do you feel the new Cold War will be focused online or offline?

CHAPTER 4

WHAT ADVOCACY ORGANIZATIONS SAY

The Cold War gave rise to a number of advocacy groups and causes, including calls for nuclear disarmament and greater human rights accountability in the international community. Already, the new Cold War is doing the same, raising concerns across a range of issues that are driving action. From social media as a tool of political propaganda to the state of national sovereignty, advocacy groups are asking important questions and posing solutions based on the changed nature of the world order and roles of Russia and the United States. Elsewhere, groups are shaping policy through specific avenues, like media access, which influences the way they view the spectre of a new Cold War.

"CAN A RUSSIAN-FUNDED CABLE NETWORK ACTUALLY PROMOTE FREE PRESS IN THE U.S.?," BY SOPHIA A. MCCLENNEN, FROM *THE CONVERSATION*, MARCH 29, 2016

With the recently announced shutdown of Al Jazeera America, the alternative cable news scene is in flux.

Launched as a corrective to the politicized and spectacle-heavy programming of Fox News, CNN and MSNBC, Al Jazeera America positioned itself as a fact-based, unbiased news source. Even though the network won awards for reporting, the Qatari government-funded channel suffered from the public perception that it had an anti-Western, pro-Islamic stance. Amid lowering gas prices and reports of other financial woes, the channel announced it would shut down its U.S. operations at the end of April.

As Al Jazeera America closes shop, it's worth wondering how this change will affect the position of RT America – previously known as Russia Today America – in the U.S. market. Like Al Jazeera, RT America has fashioned itself as a serious alternative to the politicized media circus promoted by the top three cable news stations. Unlike Al Jazeera, it runs ad-free, which arguably gives it even more potential for influence-free programming.

But RT America has some inherent contradictions: it offers a "Russian state perspective" in its news programming while simultaneously airing some of the most progressive shows on U.S. cable. As Julia Ioffe writes in the Columbia Journalism Review, RT America often acts as a "shrill propaganda outlet" for the Kremlin

– an identity that clashes with its desire to compete in the international news market.

At the same time, according to Ioffe, RT America understands that in order to effectively compete with other progressive, unbiased networks, it needs "to be taken seriously." This realization, she explains, has led to some good reporting.

It's a crazy notion – and a bit mind-boggling to consider – but RT America might be offering some of the most progressive, uncensored cable media programming in the U.S. today.

Certainly some will not be able to look past the paradox that a nation that has one of the lowest scores on the press freedom index could also be funding a valuable alternative to mainstream cable news.

But when it comes to distorting the news, is the network any more culpable than mainstream cable networks? And can U.S. audiences overcome their inherent prejudice that RT America is just a propaganda arm for the Russian government?

THE RT AMERICA PARADOX

Thus far, most coverage of RT America has focused on its ties to the Kremlin. But there's a distinct difference between the news arm of the Moscow-based Russia Today and RT America's opinion shows.

In short, the opinion and talk shows that populate RT America seem to have editorial freedom, while the news arm of RT does not.

One stark example took place over coverage of the conflict between Russia and the Ukraine.

RT news anchor Liz Wahl resigned on air, citing disagreements with RT's editorial policy. More recently, Moscow-based Sarah Firth – who worked for RT, not RT America – resigned in protest over the way that the network was covering the Malaysian Airlines crash in Ukraine.

In contrast, Abby Martin, former host of "Breaking the Set," an opinion show that aired on RT America from 2012 to 2015, openly criticized Russian military intervention into Ukraine in March of 2014. Yet she went on to continue to host her show for another year before moving on. In a note for Media Roots, she explained she was leaving the show to pursue more investigative reporting and added "RT has given me opportunities I will be eternally thankful for."

This suggests a divide at RT America over freedom of expression in opinion shows versus news coverage. It's a distinction that is important to note and to critique. But it's also one that suggests that the assumption that all RT America programming is tainted by propaganda may itself be an unfounded bias.

THE RT DIFFERENCE

While Al Jazeera America and RT America both angled to offer an alternative to mainstream U.S. news media, there are many ways that RT has followed a different – and potentially more successful – path.

First, RT America made the smart move to remove Russia from its name. Al Jazeera refused to adjust its name to appeal to U.S. viewers and distance itself from its financial backers.

RT America has also differed radically in the sort of programming offered. Balancing out its daily news programming, RT America airs analysis and commentary shows by Larry King, Thom Hartmann, Jesse Ventura and former MSNBC host Ed Schultz – all established personalities with significant appeal to American audiences.

In addition, RT America has carved out a niche with millennial viewers, with two shows aimed at a younger audience and hosted by younger talent. The first, "Watching the Hawks," is a news magazine show hosted by Tyrel Ventura (Jesse's son), Sean Stone (Oliver's son) and Tabetha Wallace.

When they were announced as new hosts for a show on RT, many dismissed the development. Wallace told me, for instance, that she is often derogatorily called "Putin's princess," since it's assumed the Russian leader controls her.

But I believe "Watching the Hawks" has fed viewers a consistent diet of cutting-edge stories on politics, media and culture. They often target corporate abuse, like pieces they've run on HSBC and Dow-Dupont.

Meanwhile, Wallace has reported on the annual gathering of veterans called "The Bikers of Rolling Thunder," and she covered the 70th Hiroshima Peace Ceremony. In my opinion, both segments are solid examples of stories that had been largely ignored in the mainstream U.S. media.

The second millennial-oriented show on RT America is "Redacted Tonight," a satirical news program hosted by political comedian Lee Camp.

Camp – described by Salon as "Jon Stewart with sharper teeth" – appeals to an audience that has become increasingly dissatisfied with mainstream news.

Since 9/11, satire news has increasingly been taken more seriously than "real" news (even though it doesn't exactly live up to that standard). Nonetheless, Jon Stewart was voted most trusted journalist after Walter Cronkite died. And viewers of "The Daily Show" and "The Colbert Report" scored higher than viewers of network news in knowledge of public issues.

Taking advantage of the fact that RT airs no advertising, Camp goes after any and all corporate and political malfeasance he can uncover. And he makes his audience laugh while doing it.

Recent episodes highlighted how the media claimed Hillary Clinton won the first Democratic debate even though Bernie Sanders won every poll, and pointed to the ongoing inability of the U.S. public to have a meaningful conversation about Israel and Palestine.

These sorts of shows were missing on Al Jazeera America. The network never attempted to break into the "fake news" market, despite the fact that it's a growing source of news and entertainment for young viewers. Nor did they provide the sort of hip, inquisitive programming found on "Watching the Hawks."

Arguably, these two shows could build a young base of viewers for RT America.

A NETWORK OF INDEPENDENT PERSONALITIES

While skeptics may think that these shows can't possibly be free of Kremlin influence, many of the top-billed hosts for RT America – Larry King, Jesse Ventura, Thom Hartmann and Ed Schultz – all share a history of being independent thinkers.

Take Thom Hartmann's show, "The Big Picture." Hartmann, a radio and TV personality and author of over 25 books, has made his career as a progressive political commentator. His two writers work in RT America's Washington, D.C. studio, and they both told me that they have zero restrictions on what they cover each night.

When I asked Hartmann, he said, "No one at RT has ever told me what to say and what not to say."

Meanwhile he explained that in any given week, "The Big Picture," covers at least three stories that simply would never appear on mainstream cable news. And yet, despite the fact that "The Big Picture" also airs on the progressive cable network Free Speech TV, his presence on RT America has to contend with assumptions of censorship and control.

King has also done a series of interviews where he's had to justify his ties to the network. In each case, he has explained that he hates censorship and that his own show is completely free of any editorial control. He has also openly disagreed with Russian policies: "I certainly vehemently disagree with the position they take on homosexuals – that's absurd to me."

No one asks anchors on NBC how it feels to work for a weapons contractor. Numerous studies, including one out of the University of Michigan, have shown that the link between GE and NBC has led to biased reporting.

Not only is the U.S. media influenced by corporations; it's also influenced by the federal government.

In 2006, journalists Amy and David Goodman reported that "Under the Bush administration, at least 20 federal agencies … spent $250 million creating hundreds of fake television news segments that [were] sent to local stations." They also documented how the government paid journalists in Iraq for positive reporting, and provided canned videos to air on cable news.

Given these examples of political and corporate influence on mainstream networks, it is worth wondering why RT gets criticized for bias while other networks get a free pass.

Lee Camp says he was drawn to RT in the first place precisely because of the editorial freedom. He knew he wouldn't have to worry about pressure from advertisers.

As he explained in the opening of one episode:

People [ask] me why Redacted Tonight is on RT and not another network...I'll tell you why. My anti-consumerism, anti-two-party-corporate-total-itarianism isn't exactly welcomed with open arms on networks showing 24/7 Wal-Mart ads.

A NEW CULTURAL COLD WAR?

RT America has certainly embraced its paradoxical role of pushing media boundaries in the U.S. that likely wouldn't be tolerated on Russian soil. But before we fall into Cold War dichotomies of U.S. press freedom and Russian media censorship, it's important to note two key realities in the 21st-century media landscape.

First, while it's important to hold RT America accountable for its coverage of Russia's intervention into Ukraine, it's worth noting that the U.S. media could equally be held accountable for its own coverage of the 9/11 attacks and the lead-up to the U.S.-Iraq War.

In 2015, four out of 10 Americans still believed there were weapons of mass destruction found in Iraq – a level of disinformation that requires media compliance. These statistics show the long-lasting impact of media bias in shaping public opinion.

Furthermore, the current U.S. news media is filled not only with bias but also with outright lies. Fox News, the most-watched cable news network, lies about 60 percent of the time, according to Politifact. For NBC and MSNBC, the score isn't much better: 46 percent.

One wonders how RT America would compare.

1. Explain the role of RT America in the cable news industry. What are the benefits and drawbacks?

2. What does the author argue in regards to RT's role in the new Cold War?

"U.S. NEEDS TO THINK TWICE BEFORE REPRISING THE COLD WAR," BY RACHELLE MARSHALL, FROM *FOREIGN POLICY IN FOCUS*, FEBRUARY 9, 2016

Not long after World War II, newspaper maps began showing Eastern Europe entirely colored in red, and political cartoons showed the red spreading across western Europe. Those who remembered those days were bound to have flashbacks last week. On February 2, President Obama announced plans to add $3.4 billion to this year's military budget request for Europe, more than quadrupling the $789 million currently budgeted for Europe. According to the *New York Times*, the West will eventually spend a whopping $40 billion on building up Ukraine's defenses against possible threats from Russia.

Administration officials said the decision reflects "a new situation, where Russia has become a more difficult actor." That situation apparently consists of Russia's annexation of Crimea two years ago, and its support for pro-Russian separatists in Ukraine. Both regions had longstanding ties to Russia, including a common language. There is no evidence that Russia intends to invade others of its neighbors, yet the same fear mongering that once prompted warnings of the Soviet Union's intent to take over all of Europe has returned. Ukraine is seemingly the first line of defense.

In January 2013, Ukraine's pro-Russian president, Viktor Yanukovych was overthrown and replaced by Petro Poroshenko in a coup carried out by an unlikely combination of pro-democracy and neo-fascist factions. It was undoubtedly no coincidence that Assistant Secretary of State for Europe Victoria Nuland had made three trips to Ukraine in the five weeks preceding the coup. Yanukovych had earlier elected to join Russia's Common Union, and as Nuland later reported, during her visits she had urged him "to turn away from Russia and get back into Europe. He had apparently declined to cooperate.

The additional military spending by the U.S. will go toward deploying weapons, tanks, and other military equipment in Hungary, Rumania, and the Baltic states, and to adding a fully armored combat brigade to existing NATO forces in the region. Administration officials said the new deployments would not violate the NATO-Russia Founding Act under which both sides pledged not to station large numbers of troops along their borders. How the Russians will view them is another matter.

It is only too easy to imagine what the American reaction would be if a large number of Russian troops were stationed in northern Mexico or Toronto. It's seems only logical that what one side regards as a defensive action, the other will see as preparation for an offensive move. As Evelyn N. Farkas, until recently the Pentagon's top official on Russia, commented, "The Russians are going to have a cow."

Meanwhile the former Soviet republic that NATO is defending from Russia shows signs of imploding, as those who hope to reform a deeply corrupt system clash with backers of a tacit agreement to cooperate with businessmen in exchange for their support against pro-Russian forces. On February 3 Ukraine's economics minister, Aivaras Abroma-vicius, resigned in protest against pressure on his ministry from powerful business interests with ties to Poroshenko. The corrupt insiders whose domination of the economy inspired mass protests in Ukraine two years ago are again members of the government.

At one point the tensions between reformers and supporters of the oligarchs erupted into a water fight. At a cabinet meeting on February 3, Interior minister Arsen B. Avakov, who is also a banker and businessman, was delivering a speech about privatizing state assets when the reformist governor of the Odessa region, Mikheil Saakashvili, broke in and accused Avakov of being a thief. "Blah, blah, blah," Avakov responded. "Blah, blah, blah," Saakashvili replied, and repeated his charge of thievery. With that, Avakov hurled a glass of water at Saakashvili — by mistake hitting the Ukrainian foreign minister instead.

It would be difficult to defend Russian president Vladimir Putin, whose dedication to democracy and justice is highly doubtful, but as the U.S. again allies itself with questionable partners, and builds up military bases close to Russia's borders, Putin has a legitimate reason to worry. More ominously, he has reason to undertake his own defensive action. Whatever form it takes, tensions between the two powers threaten to return us to the bad old days, when the two countries waged surrogate wars in Africa and South America and fears of a global war ran high.

Obama's recent decision to modernize and add to America's nuclear stockpile can only add to those fears. The decision may turn out to be either a gigantic waste of money or a forecast that the renewed Cold War will not have as peaceful an ending as the first. Putin is not the only one with reason to worry.

1. How does the author describe the Cold War period? What are the lessons the author argues we should learn?

2. What, according to the author, makes the new Cold War different from the first?

"DEBUNKING RUSSIA'S FAKE POPULAR STRUGGLE IN UKRAINE," BY ANASTASIA VLADIMIROVA, FROM *WAGING NON-VIOLENCE*, OCTOBER 13, 2015

A large animated crowd of pro-Russian demonstrators gathered outside the Kharkiv city council building in eastern Ukraine, watching and cheering as a young man in his mid-20's, wearing a green military-style jacket, took down the Ukrainian flag at the top of the building and replaced it with a Russian flag. The startling action took place on March 1, 2014, just months after massive protests against President Victor Yanukovych's decision to abandon an agreement on closer ties with the European Union — in favor of greater cooperation with Russia — had filled Independence Square in Kiev.

Yet, when news about the citizen of Kharkiv raising the Russian flag over the city council building appeared on the Internet later that day, ordinary Ukrainians had many reasons to doubt the demonstration was real. After all, the Kremlin had been waging a hybrid war against Ukraine to discredit the wave of pro-Europe protests, known as Euromaidan, since they began in November 2013.

A week later, StopFake.org, a website run by Ukrainian journalists aiming to refute distorted information about the events in Ukraine, discovered that Kharkiv's pro-Russian demonstration was likely staged. The Ukrainian activist holding the Russian flag on top of the city council building turned out to be a young Russian man from Saint Petersburg named Michael Ronkainen. StopFake reported that the Russian activist outed himself in a picture he posted to his Vkontakte page (a Russian analogue of Facebook).

According to Tetiana Matychak, the editor-in-chief of StopFake, it was readers who brought the story to the journalists' attention — specifically those from Eastern Ukraine, who were aware of Russia's efforts at deception. "We were surprised, but we checked the information very carefully and concluded that our readers were right," Matychak said.

After the "Kharkiv activist" was exposed, more readers began sending tips to StopFake, including one about a Russian flag being raised in Donetsk at a pro-Russian rally, where participants seized the regional council building. StopFake, with help from its readers, soon discovered that the activist holding the flag, Rostislav Zhuravlev, came from the Russian city of Ekaterinburg and was a friend of the self-proclaimed governor of the Donetsk region.

Zhuravlev's social media was also filled with anti-Ukrainian propaganda, with many of his posts calling on readers to liberate Novorossiya, the Eastern Ukraine region that fell into the hands of pro-Russian rebels and separatists shortly after the Euromaidan protests. These rebels seek to recruit young men to voluntarily join the fight in Eastern Ukraine. Ronkainen, for instance, posted a photo on Instagram with a police officer he met at Los Angeles International Airport, accompanied by the comment: "I met a cool guy [named] John. After his shift is over, John promised to go to Donetsk to fight for Novorossiya."

The stories of these two Russian activists are just a few of the fakes among a broader range of false information and propaganda about the situation in Ukraine produced mostly by the Russian mainstream media. For more than a year now, journalists and activists from Stop-Fake have tried to debunk distorted information and identify made-up reports and commentary through careful verification and fact checking.

"If we find 100 percent proof that the news is a fake, we write an article about it," Matychak explained. "We discuss all the topics together, but I make the final decision if this news is worth debunking or not, and if the story is worth being published."

When Matychak and her colleagues started StopFake, they only intended to run the website for two or three months, but the propaganda quickly increased and spread out of control, such that they could not let it go unanswered.

"We see the statistics," she said. "A lot of fakes come from Russian media seeking to create propaganda about the enemies of the Russian Federation – Ukraine, Georgia, NATO, the United States. These countries and organizations are not the real enemies of Russia, but the Kremlin propaganda calls them 'enemies' in order to persuade the Russian people. I can say for sure that Ukraine was not going to attack Russia and Ukraine only fights back now."

Matychak is convinced that the Kremlin-sponsored propaganda inspires pro-Russian activists to take part in staged protests pretending to be Ukrainian citizens. "Many people who came from Russia, came to Kharkiv, Donetsk and Luhansk," Matychak said. "That is the difference between Kiev protests and Eastern Ukraine protests. In Eastern Ukraine there were a lot of Russian protesters. Those people watched Russian TV channels and heard stories about Ukrainians and Junta."

THE 'MIRROR IMAGE' OF MAIDAN

According to Nataliya Gumenyuk, a Ukrainian journalist and co-founder of online news station Hromadske TV, pro-Russian activists have used a number of nonviolent tactics, including occupations and barricades, to create the perception that they are engaged in popular struggle similar to that of the protesters in Maidan, the central square in Kiev. Even though pro-Russian activists were occasionally able to make their protests appear peaceful and resemble the nonviolent atmosphere of Maidan, some of the most important aspects of nonviolent struggle were missing — namely spontaneity and authenticity, as Gumenyuk explained.

In a 2014 webinar about the Maidan Revolution produced by the International Center on Nonviolent Conflict, Gumenyuk elaborated on several other ways pro-Russian activists have mirrored the actions of their Maidan counterparts. "There have been reports of protesters who came from the villages and stayed in the tent city in Luhansk — for publicity purposes — only to return home in the evening after the cameras were gone," she said. Meanwhile, the barricades in Donetsk are "poorly constructed and serve no practical purpose, especially considering they are guarded by armed men." This is in contrast to the ones at Maidan, which were created to stop the crackdown on protesters by police.

In one particularly ridiculous incident, according to Gumenyuk, some people in Donetsk donated warm winter clothes to the so-called protesters — just as Maidan supporters had done for people protesting in Kiev during the winter months. The difference, however, was that the pro-Russian donations "took place in April, when the weather was much warmer and winter clothes were not needed."

Such actions led to the creation of what Gumenyuk referred to as "the 'mirror image' of Maidan, an attempt to give legitimacy to the pro-Russian resistance movement. Unlike the staged protests in Eastern Ukraine, however, Maidan was an authentic grassroots movement. According to Gumenyuk, people followed the genuine spirit of the protest present at Maidan, which the staged pro-Russian protests always lacked.

Nevertheless, the Russian propaganda machine is learning lessons from its public outing. "After publishing those and other stories," Matychak explained, "Russian activists in Ukraine became more careful and wise. Many of them stopped publishing selfies in social networks, for example."

MISAPPROPRIATION OF NONVIOLENT TACTICS

According to Jamila Raqib, executive director of the Albert Einstein Institution, a Boston-based non-profit devoted to advancing the study of nonviolent action, "Governments and others have, historically, tried to undermine nonviolent movements by accusing them of being created and funded by foreign governments." Kremlin-sponsored media outlets, in particular, have played a leading role in such efforts, routinely crediting Western powers with the string of popular uprisings that took place in the early 2000s in Serbia, Georgia and Ukraine. Some outlets have focused on Albert Einstein Institution founder Gene Sharp, often considered the leading theorist on nonviolent conflict.

In a 2012 segment on the Kremlin-sponsored cable news network Russia Today, Polish political activist Mateusz Piskorski called Sharp "an ideologue," and "the man who invented the whole technology of the contemporary color revolutions," adding, "Of course, the United States is the leading power when it comes to these technologies."

In another 2012 interview, this time with Sharp himself, the Russian tabloid newspaper Komsomolskaya Pravda, asked the 87-year-old Nobel Peace Price nominee to discuss how his work was "used to disintegrate the Soviet Union." Sharp responded by saying, "If the problem of the Soviet society was that an old man could suppress it, then it means this society had very big problems."

In a report published earlier this year, civil resistance scholar Maciej Bartkowki explained that the Kremlin's preoccupation with the color revolutions stems from its fear of "a similar outburst of popular discontent in Russia." Yet, despite its efforts to delegitimize nonviolent struggle, the Kremlin recognized, as Bartkowski noted in paper published earlier this year, that "a resemblance of popular grassroots support will be important for the ultimate success of the subversive operations that Russia planned in Ukraine."

As a result, the Kremlin has relied on the political mobilization of a loyal and vocal minority in the targeted territories of Eastern Ukraine, including Donetsk and Luhansk. Bartkowski's analysis suggests that such actions "provided an effective nonviolent cover for rebels and Russian special forces, bestowing on them and their actions a façade of grassroots legitimacy."

KEEPING THE RUSSIAN POPULATION IN THE DARK

During the recent conflict in Ukraine, Putin relied heavily on the information warfare conducted in social and mainstream media. According to Barkowski, his objective was to "deceive adversaries, blur the line between reality and fantasy, drive a wedge between Western allies, and keep the Russian population itself in the dark." To that end, Putin's strategy has been extremely effective. Russia's information warfare has deceived large audiences. At the beginning of last fall, Putin's approval rating was at 88 percent. Thereafter, the financial crisis notwithstanding, 70 percent of the Russian citizens expressed support for Putin's policies in Ukraine.

In April 2014, David M. Herzenhorn, a Moscow based *New York Times* correspondent, described the Kremlin's information warfare as "an extraordinary propaganda campaign that political analysts say reflects a new brazenness on the part of Russian officials. And in recent days, it has largely succeeded — at least for Russia's domestic audience — in painting a picture of chaos and danger in Eastern Ukraine, although it was pro-Russian forces themselves who created it by seizing public buildings and setting up roadblocks."

Raqib also thinks the protests organized by pro-Russian activists in Eastern Ukraine were effective and — perhaps more alarmingly — can be seen as part of a larger global trend. "Governments are studying this," she explained. "They recognize that they need to use some elements of nonviolent struggle against nonviolent movements." This is something Raqib feels the nonviolence community needs to better understand, if it's going to find effective ways of counteracting a growing trend toward hybrid warfare.

While scholars and journalists like Gumenyuk and Bartkowski are making strides in that area, crowd-sourced media watchdog groups like StopFake are creating a noticeable impact on the frontline of the struggle. "We are fighting propaganda no matter where it comes from," Matychak said. "Our main hope is to attract the attention of foreign media organizations and encourage them to not only verify all the information no matter the source, but to also learn from our experience and protect their countries from any sort of propaganda."

Matychak believes that victory will come for the nonviolent movement in Ukraine because truth is on its side. "Ukrainians don't attack. They only defend themselves, and they try to do it using truth because liars only win in the short-term. People who use truth always win in the long-term."

1. Compare and contrast Russian disinformation usage in Ukraine and another country examined in this book.

2. Explain the dangers of propaganda and how advocates are fighting it.

"THE RUSSIA SANCTIONS ARE ABOUT CONTROLLING AMERICANS," BY JEFFREY A. TUCKER, FROM THE FOUNDATION FOR ECONOMIC EDUCATION, JULY 25, 2017

Once again, Congress is legislating sweeping sanctions on a country, this time against Russia. What is behind this? It's purely symbolic, supposedly in response to Russia's hacking and meddling ways, as if a whole country should be held responsible for the alleged actions of a few or even one, and without a shred of evidence that this is due to encouragement or support from the top. Even if it were, why should a country be blamed for the malice of its leaders?

There's no thought here put into the results (beyond scoring domestic political points).

No one really believes that Vladimir Putin is going to say or think: "True, I did a bad thing but now I see that the United States means business and is punishing my country. In light of this, I really must amend my ways, sin no more, and avoid the near occasions of sin."

SORRY, NOT SORRY

No, that's not going to happen. What happens instead is that foreigners lose some measure of access to some part of another country's culture. That means isolating a country, on the margin, and reducing the flow of information and commerce in and out. The leadership now has a scapegoat to rile up the population. Cuba, North Korea, and Iran illustrate this – and the pathetic results – precisely.

Thinking of this from a results-oriented point of view, economic sanctions – deployed by the US more than any other country, especially since 9/11 – are a failed policy. (The only real success case people can point to is South Africa in the 1980s, but reforms there were already underway long before sanctions came about, and it is even possible that sanctions only delayed them and emboldened dangerous elements.)

Putin is already crowing about how the very prospect of US sanctions shows just how messed up is the US political situation, and how much the US fears him. The prospect alone has given him bragging rights, which he craves more than anything. This contributes to his popularity – as it did for

Castro, among many others. "See how awesome I am? I'm feared by the US!"

WHO IS HELPED?

What sanctions forget is that nearly all people are subject to nationalist fervor and that every man and woman is proud of his or her country. Everyone is inclined to believe that his or her country is the best and that others are insufficiently valuing their homeland. When a foreign country inveighs against your country, the tendency is not to feel bad but rather get mad. For dictators, sanctions emanating from a foreign imperial power are a gift, an ideal scapegoat and a way to tap into a powerful source for political support. This is why sanctions so often foreshadow hot war.

WHO IS HURT?

But let's talk about a feature of sanctions hardly ever mentioned: they ensnare Americans and others who are completely innocent. This might actually be the biggest feature of sanctions. They enhance the power of government over people outside the target country, thus reducing the freedom of everyone.

All of the sanctions programs by the US are enforced by the US Treasury Department's Office of Foreign Assets Control. This office has no control over the internal affairs of any sanctioned country. It can only investigate and control people within US jurisdiction or people dealing with US companies. The power is wielded not against bad guys but rather large banking and corporate institutions with trade deals in targeted countries.

Consider Rex Tillerson, current Secretary of State and former CEO of ExxonMobil. Whatever you think of his policies, what ExxonMobil was doing in Russia during his tenure there was good for consumers and oil production generally. But during his tenure, the Texas-based company ran afoul of new sanctions on Russia.

It should have been a normal deal, a great thing for everyone, the crowning achievement of many years of preparation and negotiation. Instead, the US Treasury came to be empowered to tell an American company how it can use its own property and decision-making power. This is not freedom but intrusion by the state where it does not belong. It hurts Americans, and everyone else in a globalized economy.

SEIZING FUNDS

And let's talk about Elliott Smith, a programmer from the UK who was traveling in Cuba recently. He checked his Coinbase application on his smartphone to see his earnings, and then closed it again. He did not buy or sell or otherwise adjust his account. However, the location of his phone was delivered to the merchant.

Then he received the following message.

> We have reason to believe that you reside in a country in which Coinbase is prohibited by law from doing business (Cuba) per the sanctions imposed by the U.S Treasury Department's Office of Foreign Assets Control. As a result, we've unfortunately had to close your Coinbase account.
>
> If you are not a resident of a sanctioned country or otherwise have received this notification in error,

please contact us...immediately and provide us with a copy of a photo ID and proof of your current address.

If your account has a balance you will need to contact the U.S. Treasury Department to request permission to access your funds.

In short, in the name of sanctions enforcement, all his money was stolen by the US government, even though he is a UK citizen. More than two months later, he has yet to get his money or account back. This is done in the name of enforcing sanctions against Cuba but no one in Cuba felt this action. The coercive power of the state was felt only by an innocent bystander.

Here is a clear illustration of the point. Sanctions are about controlling people, not so much in the target country where there is no jurisdiction, but rather those who are trading with people in the target country. It's coercion against innocents, a regulatory tax on enterprise. That's the only way they are enforced.

In the case of Russia, a country very much part of the world economic order, US sanctions will ensnare not only US companies but European ones as well. So it is not surprising that the European Union is planning some strategy of resistance to protect industrial and financial interests in Europe.

All this muscle is being applied toward what end? To "punish" Russia. But the Russian state will not be punished (quite the opposite), but the Russian people: and not only the Russian people. People working and trading with people in the Russian jurisdiction will be punished for no good reason. And all of this is being pushed for – Putin is sadly correct here – domestic political reasons.

The US wants to look tough in a standoff against Russia, but Putin laughs it off, government power over merchants and traders intensifies, and the growth of global commerce – the best means by which the world realizes peace and prosperity – is hobbled yet again.

Anyone agree that the Republican Congress would be better off spending time cutting taxes, reducing regulations, or abolishing Obamacare, and other things that might increase people's liberties rather than increase government control over our commercial dealings?

1. How does the author argue sanctions against Russia will hurt Americans?

2. Based on this article, describe the economic relationship between Russia and the United States, and how that might be impacted by a cold war.

CHAPTER 5

WHAT THE MEDIA SAY

Reporting on Russia–United States relations has always been a media focus, but that attention has increased in the wake of the 2016 election. Today, media professionals are paying even closer attention to Russia and the United States, as well as to China and changing relations between the three. This is good and bad; although the increased reporting can provide a wider understanding of relations between these nations, it can also create a false sense of increased tension or panic. This can make it seem like there is a greater risk of conflict than there truly is, making it important to keep in mind context and history for Russia–United States relations.

"NO GOOD CAN COME FROM TRYING TO RESURRECT THE COLD WAR," BY BRITTANY HUNTER, FROM THE FOUNDATION FOR ECONOMIC EDUCATION, MAY 29, 2017

A few days go, as I sat with my eyes fixated on my television screen during a particularly riveting Netflix marathon, an alert on my iPhone went off and interrupted an otherwise perfect night of binge-watching.

As I glanced down to see what fresh new hell awaited me in the hectic non-fiction world, I noticed that it was an alert from an Apple news app that I never bothered to deleted when I upgraded to a newer iPhone over six months ago. The app only goes off if there is significant breaking news, which, usually means a terrorist attack or another lost airliner.

This time, however, the news that disrupted my luxurious night of lounging was a headline about Jared Kushner, Trump's loyal son-in-law, and his connection to Russia. The content of the alert was vague at best, something along the lines of "Kushner has Russian connection Proving Malicious Intent," or something equally over-dramatic and sensationalized.

ENOUGH IS ENOUGH

Normally, I would roll my eyes at the media rushing to conclusions and go about my day, but after the roller coaster of an election cycle that the nation is still attempting to recover from, this alert somehow managed to become my own personal "straw that broke the camel's back," as they say.

For the record, I am no fan of Jared Kushner nor of Trump, but that is because I am no fan of any politician. However, given the amount of times I have personally been subjected to the " fear Russia" rhetoric, I find myself quickly losing faith in what passes for "news" these days and am even more concerned that this fear mongering will inevitably turn to warmongering if the drums of war continue to beat in Russia's general direction.

Between hearing the term "Russian meddling" every 30 seconds on CNN, and *Time* Magazine's controversial cover depicting the White House being taken over by the Kremlin, I have had just about enough of this return to 1950s Cold War speak.

While I am wary of any news story that justifies the military industrial complex's lust for war, the *Time* cover speaks volumes about the modern day media industry as a whole. When it comes to the purposefully shocking Time cover, no one bothered to notice that the "Kremlin" seen swallowing the White House into a sea of red is in fact St. Basil Cathedral. The sensationalism of the story, despite its possible consequences, was of more importance than fact-checking the actual content.

Some might argue that this is a small detail to get worked up over in the long-run, but as the country "celebrates" Memorial Day today, it is important to remember that any rhetoric that aims to perpetuate our country's obsession with war should always be questioned and scrutinized to the utmost degree.

REINVENTING THE RED SCARE

Russia has recently replaced the millennial generation as America's favorite group to collectively throw under the bus every time something goes wrong.

At a pivotal moment just a few weeks shy of voting day, Wikileaks revealed leaked emails that showed collusion between the Democratic National Committee (DNC) and the Hillary Clinton campaign (as if either can be distinguished from the other). The content of these emails seemed to shed light on the combined efforts of the DNC and the Clinton campaign, who together had done everything within their power to rig the election against Bernie Sanders.

But rather than blame those actually responsible for the constructed demise of the Sanders campaign, Russia somehow became the enemy — again.

Suddenly, the shadiness on the part of the DNC and the Clinton camp were pushed aside as "Russian hackers" became the main cause for concern. While there has yet to be a definitive answer on the matter, the authenticity of the leaked emails was not a source of outrage for devoted Democrats. Instead, they wanted justice because how dare we let Putin interfere in our elections! This is America! This is a Democracy!

Overnight, the Democrats began to sound like the bloodthirsty Republicans of the Bush/Cheney era, calling for war without any logical forethought. What their candidate did was of less importance than punishing those who may or may not have brought the information to light.

Appearing almost out of thin air, Russia became the culprit even though there was evidence to the contrary and Wikileaks maintains that Russia is not involved. For those insistent that the Red Scare be brought forth from its warmongering grave, the idea of a foreign body meddling in the U.S. presidential elections was too egregious a reality to live with in an allegedly free country.

Apparently, these same people have forgotten about the numerous times throughout history where the United States Government has interfered in foreign elections over the years.

BLOOD ON OUR HANDS

If for example, Russia was found to be explicitly and directly tied to the election of Donald Trump, it does not, at least thus far, come close to the disastrous consequences that arose from America's role in the Iranian coup d'etat in 1953. It also pales in comparison with the American backing of the President of the Republic of Vietnam, Ngo Dinh Diem in the 1960s. In the predominantly Buddhist territory of southern Vietnam, the United States ushering a devout Catholic into the powerful role of President was not appreciated, as history proved.

While these are just a few instances of many, the aforementioned examples have both caused and perpetuated conflicts that are still ongoing today. The United State's reputation of meddling in the Middle East is exactly what gave rise to the sentiment seen with Islamist extremists, such as Isis. But it didn't begin in 2003 with the Invasion of Iraq.

The United States left Vietnam in shame after forcing their own men to go off and die in foreign jungles without a clear purpose. But U.S. intervention was largely to blame for the escalation of the conflict in the first time.

Simply knowing and understanding that the state has an unfortunate tendency of being all too hasty to declare war — or just attack without any formal declaration — should be enough to caution those who are calling for the nation to retaliate against Russia.

LET'S REALLY REMEMBER

Memorial Day has unfortunately become a holiday that glamorizes war and glorifies professional state-sanctioned killing, rather than urging caution against escalating foreign conflict. While the U.S. Department of Veterans Affairs (VA) has been an utter and complete disaster when it comes to honoring those who went off to die for undefined "American interests" abroad, the government has instead declared that Memorial Day is sufficient enough to at least calm the masses.

But as we spend the majority of the day enjoying our paid time off with BBQs and pool time, may we not forget to be increasingly skeptical of any propaganda that seeks to put the state's interests ahead of individual life.

To be sure, the atrocities committed by Putin and other Russian agents of the state are reprehensible. However, not only does this not explicitly prove that Russia was involved in the leaks, those seeking to perpetuate this rhetoric are doing so only to save face and distract from the actions of the DNC and the Clinton camp.

For those who continue attempting to reignite the Cold War, protecting partisan politics is more important than sparing innocent lives from the brutal realities of war.

1. Why does the author argue that politicians should avoid beginning a new Cold War?

2. What alternatives does she present as ways to respond to Russia?

"RUSSIA FIGHTING INFORMATION WARS WITH BORROWED WEAPONS," BY CYNTHIA HOOPER, FROM *THE CONVERSATION*, MARCH 30, 2015

"Life would be boring without rumors."

So said Russian President Vladimir Putin, upon re-emerging from a mysterious ten-day disappearance, during which the internet exploded with speculation he was dead.

The Kremlin added fuel to the fire after posting photos of Putin on its website it claimed were current – but which turned out to have been images from a meeting that had taken place a week earlier.

It's not the first time that Putin and the Kremlin have played fast and loose with the facts. At the annual G-20 summit in Australia last fall, when the Prime Minister of Canada told Putin to get his country's troops out of Ukraine, the Russian leader apparently responded, "Unfortunately, this cannot be done, as we are not there." (And remember the "little green men" in Crimea whom Putin suggested were not Russian soldiers, but unknown citizens masquerading in used Russian uniforms?)

Yet according to polls, 85% of Russians voters trust Putin, an all-time high. And even though it's common knowledge that the state has seized control of the country's three main television stations, somewhere between 80% and 90% of citizens continue to rely on those stations for their news. (Russians watch an average of 3 ½ hours of state TV a day.)

Why are Russians so willing to swallow misinformation? Have the country's citizens – after decades of learning to read between the lines during the Soviet era – suddenly become gullible?

Not exactly. Instead, the Kremlin has become increasingly sophisticated in its media strategy.

Even as it continues to enforce conformity of coverage at home, it criticizes conformity abroad. Moreover, it borrows from the playbook of its former Cold War enemy, the US, to shape public opinion – in part by concocting a powerful story of Western spin.

NEWSPEAKING FROM BOTH SIDES OF THE MOUTH

To the international audience, the Kremlin advertises pro-Russian coverage as an "alternative point of view" that any truly "free" press should acknowledge.

"Question More" reads the slogan of the Kremlin's English-language news service Russia Today (RT).

Such rhetoric borrows heavily from that of Fox News. Upon launching in 1996, the nascent network introduced itself to US viewers as a "Fair and Balanced" alternative to what it claimed was the country's overwhelming "liberal media bias."

Likewise, in selling their product as more open-minded alternative to the supposed "Anglo-Saxon mass-media monopoly," RT has enjoyed astonishing success.

Last November, the government went even further, announcing the formation of a new global media service named Sputnik to challenge US-led "aggressive propaganda promoting a unipolar world."

These media agencies are slick – and not stupid.

In particular, their criticism of the American political establishment is often hard-hitting, conveying concerns about US-led hegemony shared by other countries across the world.

Such outlets typically argue that the US media frames the Ukraine conflict in outdated Cold War clichés, and that it too readily embraces Ukrainian leaders who are also manipulating information to elicit Western sympathy (not to mention vast amounts of financial aid). It also argues that Western media hypocritically avoids probing into the United States' own checkered record of overseas crimes.

"We've switched roles," crowed Sputnik chief Dmitry Kiselev last year. "Russia is for freedom of expression and the West is not."

A WESTERN TOOLBOX

Some accuse the Kremlin of "weaponizing information," combining the Newspeak of George Orwell with "the savvy of Don Draper." According to journalists Peter Pomerantsev and Michael Weiss, Russian "political technologists" work behind the scenes to insert deliberately false material into international public debate in the name of balanced and objective coverage.

At the same time, they strive to discredit the very principle of objectivity, encouraging viewers to believe that – especially during international conflicts – all journalism is skewed by politics and preconceptions.

It's a deeply cynical strategy. But it works. Most Russians appear to embrace the argument that "everybody lies" – including the West.

"Isn't the labeling that CNN and BBC use also propaganda?" opinedleading Russian state television anchor Andrei Kondrashov. "We [in Russia] have simply adopted the same methods that they use today."

Kondrashov and others point out that US corporations and Hollywood celebrities (not to mention US presidential candidates) all hire expensive PR firms to place stories, tactically leak information and cultivate point people who can be relied upon for appropriate spin. And, indeed, a recent report from the Bureau of Labor Statistics predicts a decrease of 7,200 journalism jobs by 2022, but an increase of 27,400 positions in PR.

Then there's the mass hiring of internet trolls to articulate a pro-Putin message on Western media sites. Many US journalists have called it a "Kremlin attack" to "claim control over the internet." Moderators at the British *Guardian* – where articles can be flooded with as many as 40,000 comments a day – have termed it an "orchestrated campaign." Meanwhile, the English-language *Moscow Times* has been forced to shut down its online discussion forum, citing floods of spam.

Russia's only remaining independent investigative newspaper interviewed individuals who admitted to being paid to produce a quota of 100 posts a day. But in explaining their responsibilities, the interviewees echoed the language of US election campaign managerswho organize "rapid response" teams of volunteers to write letters to the editor, post on social media and comment on articles – all to shape and influence debate.

ENTERTAINMENT'S AGENDA

Russian celebrities also play a role in molding public opinion.

Director Nikita Mikhalkov, for instance, is a long-time critic of Soviet-style dictatorship. (He won an Oscar for his anti-Stalin 1995 film *Burnt By the Sun.*) Yet he's also an outspoken Russian nationalist – and a close friend of Putin. At the premier of his most recent film, Mikhalkov declared, "Anyone who says Crimea is not Russian is the enemy."

His next project will be a television series about the death of legendary 19th century Russian writer-diplomat Aleksandr Griboedov. The director claims that he will correct the historical record, to "prove" that Griboedov was killed in Tehran by Muslims acting under the direction of British spies during a time of Anglo-Russian competition for influence in Central Asia.

Though set in the distant past, the project reinforces contemporary media messages: just as the British connived to undermine Russian interests in 19th-century Persia, so, too, are the Americans meddling in Ukraine.

But US popular culture is also filled with anti-Russian allusions. For example, the third season of *House of Cards* depicts US President Frank Underwood locking horns with his Russian counterpart, Viktor Petrov – a figure who shares not only the same initials as his real-life model, but also a KGB background, an extended term in office, a failed marriage and a penchant for political cynicism.

"Russia has nothing to gain from peace in the Middle East and, more importantly, nothing to gain from working with America," Petrov intones in one episode, minutes after being received at the White House.

Meanwhile NBC's *Allegiance* centers on Russian spies in America who are plotting a terrorist operation to retaliate against US sanctions. It's an attack that will, exults one character, "allow us to operate as we wish, in Ukraine, in Europe, in the world."

One early scene depicts the plotters slowly feeding one of their colleagues suspected of betrayal into a furnace, after reminding him that the name of their organization may have changed but "the rules remain the same."

Viewers are thereby encouraged to link contemporary Russian intelligence operatives to the Soviet-era KGB, with a twist of modern-day ISIS thrown in.

STILL, RUSSIA'S IN A LEAGUE OF ITS OWN

But differences in degrees of media freedom matter, and borrowed strategies do not mean equivalent ones. What's important is to find a way to criticize the shortcomings of US media practice and policy, without fully embracing Russian spin.

While both countries may be promoting a "new Cold War" along cultural lines, what distinguishes Russia is the level of manipulation involved in, as Putin's critics phrase it, "activating hatred."

It's a process fueled by an increasingly organized, largely invisible set of censorship personnel and practices. Government pressure on the handful of independent outlets that remain continues to grow. (The haunting question of who's behind the death of opposition leader Boris Nemtsov looms large.)

Meanwhile, the most popular programs remain the ones where fact and fiction unapologetically blur.

A self-described "documentary film" that aired in mid-March to commemorate the first anniversary of Russia's annexation of the Crimea opens with a shot of a Russian Orthodox church, a military helicopter and an interview with Putin.

Crimea: The Way Home first aired in mid-March and has already garnered over 5 million views.

"I invited the head of Special Operations to the Kremlin," Putin somberly recounts, "and told him, 'let's speak directly, that we must save the life of the President of Ukraine.'"

Combining professional History Channel-style packaging with staged re-enactments of events (that may not have even taken place), the film, titled *Crimea: The Way Home* has already garnered more than five million views online.

It's a testament to the immense – and rapid – growth of Russia's mighty media megaphone.

1. Why does the author characterize Russia's use of the media as a "borrowed tool"?

2. What makes media-based propaganda dangerous? Are there any times when it could be useful?

"CHINA, AMERICA, AND A NEW COLD WAR IN AFRICA?," BY NICK TURSE, FROM *FOREIGN POLICY IN FOCUS*, AUGUST 5, 2014"

Juba, South Sudan — Is this country the first hot battlefield in a new cold war? Is the conflict tearing this new nation apart actually a proxy fight between the world's two top economic and military powers?

That's the way South Sudan's Information Minister Michael Makuei Lueth tells it. After "midwifing" South Sudan into existence with billions of dollars in assistance, aid, infrastructure projects, and military support, the United States has watched China emerge as the major beneficiary of South Sudan's oil reserves. As a result, Makuei claims, the United States and other Western powers have backed former vice president Riek Machar and his rebel forces in an effort to overthrow the country's president, Salva Kiir. China, for its part, has played a conspicuous double game. Beijing has lined up behind Kiir, even as it publicly pushes both sides to find a diplomatic solution to a simmering civil war. It is sending peacekeepers as part of the U.N. mission even as it also arms Kiir's forces with tens of millions of dollars worth of new weapons.

While experts dismiss Makuei's scenario — "farfetched" is how one analyst puts it — there are average South Sudanese who also believe that Washington supports the rebels. The United States certainly did press Kiir's government to make concessions, as his supporters are quick to remind anyone willing to listen, pushing it to release senior political figures detained as coup plotters shortly after fighting broke out in late 2013. The United States, they say, cared more about a handful of elites sitting in jail than all the South Sudanese suffering in a civil war that has now claimed more than 10,000 lives, resulted in mass rapes, displaced more than 1.5 million people (around half of them children), and pushed the country to the very brink of famine.

Opponents of Kiir are, however, quick to mention the significant quantities of Chinese weaponry flooding into the country. They ask why the United States hasn't put pressure on a president they no longer see as legitimate.

While few outside South Sudan would ascribe to Makuei's notion of a direct East-West proxy war here, his conspiracy theory should, at least, serve as a reminder that U.S. and Chinese interests are at play in this war-torn nation and across Africa as a whole — and that Africans are taking note. Almost anywhere you look on the continent, you can now find evidence of both the U.S. and the Chinese presence, although they take quite different forms. The Chinese are pursuing a ruthlessly pragmatic economic power-projection strategy with an emphasis on targeted multilateral interventions in African conflicts. U.S. policy, in contrast, appears both more muddled and more military-centric, with a heavy focus on counterterrorism efforts meant to bolster amorphous strategic interests.

For the last decade, China has used "soft power" — aid, trade, and infrastructure projects — to make major inroads on the continent. In the process, it has set itself up as the dominant foreign player here. The United States, on the other hand, increasingly confronts Africa as a "battlefield" or "battleground" or "war" in the words of the men running its operations. In recent years, there has been a substantial surge in U.S. military activities of every sort, including the setting up of military outposts and both direct and proxy interventions. These two approaches have produced starkly contrasting results for the powers involved and the rising nations of the continent. Which one triumphs may have profound implications for all parties in the years ahead. The differences are, perhaps, nowhere as stark as in the world's newest nation, South Sudan.

A MIDWIFE'S TALE

Starting in the 1980s, the efforts of an eclectic, bipartisan collection of U.S. supporters — Washington activists, evangelical Christians, influential Congressional representatives, celebrities, a rising State Department star, a presidential administration focused on regime change and nation-building, and another that picked up the mantle — helped bring South Sudan into existence. "Midwife" was the word then-chair of the Senate Foreign Relations Committee John Kerry chose to describe the process.

In recent years, no country in Africa has received as much Congressional attention. And on July 9, 2011, South Sudan's Independence Day, President Barack Obama released a stirring statement. "I am confident that the bonds of friendship between South Sudan and the United States will only deepen in the years to come. As Southern Sudanese undertake the hard work of building their new country, the United States pledges our partnership as they seek the security, development, and responsive governance that can fulfill their aspirations and respect their human rights."

As the new nation broke away from Sudan after decades of bloody civil war, the United States poured in billions of dollars in humanitarian aid and pumped in hundreds of millions of dollars of military and security assistance. It also invested heavily in governmental institutions, and built infrastructure (constructing or repairing roads and bridges). It sent military instructors to train the country's armed forces and advisors to mentor government officials. It helped to beef up the education sector, worked to facilitate economic development and American investment, and opened the U.S. market to duty-free South Sudanese imports.

The new nation, it was hoped, would bolster U.S. national security interests by injecting a heavy dose of democracy into the heart of Africa, while promoting political stability and good governance. Specifically, it was to serve as a democratic bulwark against Sudan and its president, Omar al-Bashir, who had once harbored Osama bin Laden and is wanted by the International Criminal Court for crimes against humanity in that country's Darfur region.

When South Sudan broke away, it took much of Sudan's oil wealth with it, becoming sub-Saharan Africa's third-largest oil producer behind Nigeria and Angola. In taking those resources out of Bashir's hands, it offered the promise of more energy stability in Africa. It was even expected to serve Washington's military aims — and soon, the United States began employing South Sudanese troops as proxies in a quest to destroy Joseph Kony and his murderous Lord's Resistance Army.

That was the dream, at least. But like Washington's regime change and nation-building projects in Iraq and Afghanistan, things soon started going very, very wrong. Today, South Sudan's armed forces are little more than a collection of competing militias that have fractured along ethnic lines and turned on each other. The country's political institutions and economy are in shambles, its oil production (which accounts for about 90% of government revenue) is crippled, corruption goes unchecked, towns have been looted and leveled during recent fighting, the nation is mired in a massive humanitarian crisis, famine looms, and inter-ethnic relations may have been irreparably damaged.

THE CHINA SYNDROME

During the years when the United States was helping bring South Sudan into existence, another world power also took an interest in the country — and a very different tack when it came to its development. After having invested a reported $20 billion in Sudan — a country long on the U.S. sanctions blacklist — China watched as the new nation of South Sudan claimed about 75% of its oil fields. In 2012, newly inaugurated South Sudanese President Salva Kiir traveled to China where he sipped champagne with then-President Hu Jintao and reportedly secured a pledge of $8 billion to build up his country's infrastructure and support its oil sector. (A top Chinese envoy later dismissed reports of such a sum, but hinted that China was willing to make even greater investments in the country if it achieved a lasting peace with its northern neighbor.)

Two years later, the China National Petroleum Corporation, with a 40% stake, is now the largest shareholder in the Greater Nile Petroleum Operating Company, the top oil consortium in South Sudan. It also leads another important consortium, the Greater Pioneer Operating Company.

During the first 10 months of 2013, China imported nearly 14 million barrels of oil from South Sudan. That adds up to about 77% of the country's crude oil output and twice as much as China imports from energy-rich Nigeria. While South Sudanese oil accounts for only about 5% of China's total petroleum imports, the country has nonetheless provided Beijing with a new African partner. This was especially useful as a U.S. and NATO intervention in Libya in 2011 created chaotic conditions, causing China to suffer heavy losses ($20 billion according to Chinese sources) in various energy and other projects in that country.

"At the end of the day, China's main interest is stability so that they can function on a commercial basis. And to achieve that stability they've had to get more involved on the political side," says Cameron Hudson, director for African affairs on the staff of the National Security Council at the White House from 2005 to 2009. "They have a very large presence in Juba and are doing a lot of business beyond the oil sector."

In fact, just days before South Sudan plunged into civil war late last year, the deep-pocketed Export-Import Bank of China was reportedly preparing to offer the country $2 billion in loans and credit to build six key roads — including a 1,500-mile highway to link the capital, Juba, with Sudan's main port — crucial bridges across the Nile River, schools and hospitals in every county, a hydropower plant, a government conference center, and a staple of Chinese construction schemes in Africa, a stadium.

Recently, Chinese Premier Li Keqiang promised to expand cooperation with South Sudan in trade, agriculture, construction of infrastructure, and energy. Meanwhile, a separate $158 million deal to repair and expand the airport in Juba, financed by China's Export-Import Bank and carried out by a Chinese firm, was announced. In addition, China has just shipped nearly $40 million in arms — millions of rounds of ammunition, thousands of automatic rifles and grenade launchers, and hundreds of machine guns and pistols — to Salva Kiir's armed forces.

CONTINENTAL COMPETITION

China's interest in South Sudan is indicative of its relations with the continent as a whole. Beijing has long looked to Africa for diplomatic cooperation in the international arena and, with the continent accounting for more than 25% of the votes in the General Assembly of the United Nations, relied on it for political support. More recently, economics has become the paramount factor in the growing relation-ship between the rising Asian power and the continent.

Hungry for energy reserves, minerals, and other raw materials to fuel its domestic growth, China's Export-Import Bank and other state-controlled entities regularly offer financing for railroads, highways, and other major infrastructure projects, often tied to the use of Chinese companies and workers. In exchange, China expects long-term supplies of needed natural resources. Such relationships have exploded in the new century with its African trade jumping from $10 billion to an estimated $200 billion, which far exceeds that of the United States or any European country. It has now been

Africa's largest trading partner for the last five years and boasts of having struck $400 billion worth of deals in African construction projects which have already yielded almost 1,400 miles of railroad track and nearly 2,200 miles of highways.

Resources traded for infrastructure are, however, just one facet of China's expanding economic relationship with Africa. Looking down the road, Beijing increasingly sees the continent as a market for its manufacturing products. While the West ages and sinks deeper into debt, Africa is getting younger and growing at an exponential pace. Its population is, according to demographers, poised to double by the middle of the century, jumping to as many as 3.5 billion — larger than China and India combined — with working-age people far outnumbering the elderly and children.

With its ability to produce goods at low prices, China is betting on being a major supplier of a growing African market when it comes to food, clothes, appliances, and other consumer goods. As Howard French, author of China's Second Continent notes, "a variety of economic indicators show that the fortunes of large numbers of Africans are improving dramatically and will likely continue to do so over the next decade or two, only faster." According to the International Monetary Fund, 10 of the 20 economies projected to grow fastest from 2013-2017 are located in sub-Saharan Africa. Last year, the World Bank attributed 60% of Africa's economic growth to consumer spending. Beijing may even fuel this rise further by relocating low-skilled, labor-intensive jobs to that continent as it develops more skilled manufacturing and high-tech industries at home.

One Chinese export integral to Beijing's dealings with Africa has, however, largely escaped notice. In the space of a decade, as French points out, one million or more Chinese have emigrated to Africa, buying up land, establishing businesses, plying just about every conceivable trade from medicine to farming to prostitution. These expats are altering the fundamentals of cultural and economic exchange across the continent and creating something wholly new. "For all of China's denials that its overseas ambitions could be compared to those of Europeans or Americans," writes French, "…what I was witnessing in Africa is the higgledy-piggledy cobbling together of a new Chinese realm of interest. Here were the beginnings of a new empire."

This mass influx of Chinese pioneers has bred resentment in some quarters, as have heavy-handed tactics by Chinese companies that often ignore local labor laws and environmental regulations, freeze out local workers, mistreat them, or pay them exceptionally low wages. This, in turn, has led to instances of violence against Africa's Chinese, as has Beijing's support for unpopular and repressive governments on the continent. Such threats to the safety of Chinese citizens and business interests, as well as general political instability and armed conflicts — from Libya to South Sudan — have given China still another reason to build-up its presence.

Traditionally, Beijing has adhered to a non-interference, "no strings attached" foreign policy — meaning no requirements on partner nations in terms of transparency, corruption, environmental protection, human rights, or good governance — and, as opposed to the United States, has avoided overseas military inventions. While it has long contributed to U.N. peacekeeping operations — the only kind of foreign intervention Beijing considers legitimate — China has generally operated far from the front lines. But things are subtly shifting on this score.

In 2011, after the U.S.-backed revolution in Libya imperiled 30,000 Chinese living there, the People's Liberation Army coordinated air and sea assets in the largest evacuation mission in its history. And as the war in Libya destabilized neighboring Mali and a U.S.-trained officer overthrew that country's elected president, China sent combat troops — for the first time in its history — to join U.N. forces in a bid to stabilize a nation that the United States had spent a decade bolstering through counterterrorism funding.

Then, when U.S.-backed South Sudan slid into civil war late last year — and 300 Chinese workers had to be evacuated — Beijing departed from the hands-off approach it had taken only a few years earlier with Sudan, ramped up diplomatic efforts and pushed hard for peace talks.

"This is something new for us," said China's special envoy to Africa, Zhong Jianhua. This was, he noted, the beginning of a "new chapter" in policies by which China would now "do more [in terms of] peace and security for this continent."

More recently, Beijing managed to broker an unprecedented arrangement to expand the mandate of the U.N. Mission in South Sudan. In addition to "protection of civilians, monitoring and investigating human rights abuses, and facilitating the delivery of humanitarian assistance," according to Foreign Policy, "Beijing quietly secured a deal that will put the U.N.'s famed blue helmets to work protecting workers in South Sudan's oil installations, where China has invested billions of dollars." Although protecting the oil fields is akin to taking the government's side in a civil war, the United States, France, and Great Britain backed the plan to protect oil installations under a U.N. mandate, citing the importance of the energy sector to the future of the country. In return, China will send an 850-man infantry battalion to bolster the U.N. mission, adding to the 350 military personnel it already had on the ground here.

When it comes to protecting their infrastructure, "the Chinese have gotten very good at deploying peace-keeping forces," Patricia Taft, a senior associate with the Fund for Peace, tells TomDispatch. "The Chinese have, in East Africa and also West Africa, inserted themselves as a security presence, mainly to protect their oil inter-ests, their infrastructure, or whatever economic projects they're deeply invested in."

Yun Sun, a fellow at the Stimson Center and an expert on China's relations with Africa, doesn't see these recent developments as a militarization of China's mission, but as a symptom of increased investment in the countries of the continent. "China cares more about security issues in Africa… due to its own national interests," Sun tells TomDispatch. "It means China will contribute more to the peace and security issues of the continent." And it seems that Beijing is now doing so, in part on America's dime.

WINNERS AND LOSERS

U.S. taxpayers, who fund about 27% percent of the cost of United Nations peacekeeping missions, are now effectively underwriting China's efforts to protect its oil interests in South Sudan. Washington continues to pour aid into that country — more than $456 million in humanitarian assistance in fiscal year 2014 — while China has pledged far less in humanitarian relief. Meanwhile, Juba has tied itself ever more tightly to Chinese energy interests, with plans to borrow more than $1 billion from oil companies to keep the government afloat as it battles the rebels.

Taft sees these deals with largely Chinese firms as both risky for South Sudan's future and potentially ineffective as well. "It's putting a band-aid on a hemorrhaging artery," she says. David Deng, research director for the South Sudan Law Society, echoes this: "We're mortgaging our children's future to fight a pointless war."

South Sudan seems emblematic of a larger trend in the race between Washington and Beijing in Africa. In 2000, China's trade there passed $10 billion for the first time and has been growing at a 30% clip annually ever since. Nine years later, China overtook the United States to become the continent's largest trading partner and, by 2012, its trade was nearly double that of the United States— $198.5 billion to $99.8 billion. While the United States recently announced that $900 million in unspecified "deals" with Africa will be unveiled at an upcoming U.S.-Africa Leaders Summit in Washington, it will nonetheless continue to trail far behind China in terms of trade on the continent.

For the Chinese, Africa is El Dorado, a land of opportunity for one million migrants. For the United States, it's a collection of "ungoverned spaces," "austere locations," and failing states increasingly dominated by local terror groups poised to become global threats, a danger zone to be militarily managed through special operators and proxy armies. "In Africa, terrorists, criminal organizations, militias, corrupt officials, and pirates continue to exploit ungoverned and under-governed territory on the continent and its surrounding waters," reads the Pentagon's 2014 Quadrennial Defense Review (QDR). "The potential for rapidly developing threats, particularly in fragile states, including violent public protests and terrorist attacks, could pose acute challenges to U.S. interests."

"Recent engagements in Somalia and Mali, in which African countries and regional organizations are working together with international partners in Europe and the United States, may provide a model for future partnerships," adds the QDR. But a look at those poster-child nations for U.S. involvement — one in East and one in West Africa — instead provides evidence of America's failings on the continent.

In 2006, the Islamic Court Union (ICU), a loose confederation of indigenous Islamist groups seeking to impose order on the failed state of Somalia, defeated the Alliance for Restoration of Peace and Counterterrorism, a U.S.-supported militia, and pushed the U.S.-backed warlords out of Mogadishu, the capital. In response, the United States green-lighted a 2007 invasion of the country by Ethiopia's military and secretly sent in a small contingent of its own troops (still operating in Somalia to this day). This succeeded only in splintering the ICU, sending its moderates into exile, while its hardliners formed a far more extreme Islamic group, al-Shabab, which became the key Muslim resistance force against Washington's Ethiopian proxies.

Al-Shabab experienced a great deal of military success before being beaten back by the Ethiopians, troops from a U.S.-supported Somali transitional government, and well-armed peacekeepers from the U.S.-backed African Union Mission in Somalia (AMISOM). These forces were, from 2009 onward, joined by proxies trained and armed by U.S.-ally Kenya, whose own army invaded the country in 2011. Their forces in Somalia, eventually folded into the AMISOM mission, are still deployed there. On the run and outgunned, al-Shabab responded by threatening to take the war beyond its borders and soon began to do so.

In other words, what started as a local Islamic group achieving, according to a Chatham House report, "the unthinkable, uniting Mogadishu for the first time in 16 years, and reestablishing peace and security," quickly became a transnational terror organization in the wake of the Ethiopian invasion and other acts of intervention. In 2010, al-Shabab carried out a bomb attack in Uganda as a punishment for that country's contribution to the African Union mission in Somalia. In 2011, it launched an escalating series of shootings, grenade attacks, and bombings in Kenya. The next year, the formerly Somalia-centric outfit further internationalized its efforts as one of its leaders pledged obedience to al-Qaeda chief Ayman al-Zawahiri. In 2013, the group carried out a devastating attack on the Westgate Mall in Kenya that killed 67.

Earlier this year, al-Shabab extended its reach even further with its first-ever suicide attack in Djibouti, the tiny Horn of Africa nation that contributes troops to AMISOM and hosts French troops, a key European proxy force for Washington on the continent, as well as the only avowed U.S. base in Africa. "The attack was carried out against the French Crusaders for their complicity in the massacres and persecution of our Muslim brothers in the Central African

Republic and for their active role in training and equipping the apostate Djiboutian troops in Somalia," read an al-Shabab statement that also highlighted a U.S.-backed French military mission in the Central African Republic.

In the months since, the group has repeatedly launched murderous assaults on civilians in Kenya and continues to threaten Uganda and Burundi, which also contributes troops to AMISOM, with future attacks. It has even gained regional affiliates, like Al-Hijra, an underground group accused of recruiting for al-Shabab in Kenya.

After 9/11, on the opposite side of the continent, U.S. programs like the Pan-Sahel Initiative and the Trans-Saharan Counterterrorism Partnership, pumped hundreds of millions of dollars into training and arming the militaries of Mali, Niger, Chad, Mauritania, Nigeria, Algeria, and Tunisia, again in order to promote regional "stability." While U.S. Special Operations forces were teaching infantry tactics to Malian troops, the Chinese were engaging very differently with that West African nation. Despite Mali's lack of natural resources, China constructed a key bridge, a hospital, a stadium, a major government building, several factories, miles of highways, and a $230 million waterworks project.

The United States wasn't, however, left totally out in the cold on the construction front. The State Department's Millennium Challenge Corporation (MCC), for example, spent $71.6 million to expand the Bamako Airport. The contract, however, went to a Chinese firm — as did many MCC contracts across Africa — because American companies were uninterested in working there despite guaranteed U.S. financing.

What Washington was trying to build in Mali came crashing down, however, after the United States helped topple Libyan dictator Muammar Gaddafi in 2011, causing that country to collapse into a morass of militia fiefdoms. Nomadic Tuareg fighters looted the weapons stores of the Gaddafi regime they had previously served, crossed the border, routed U.S.-backed Malian forces and seized the northern part of the country. This, in turn, prompted a U.S.-trained officer to stage a military coup in the Malian capital, Bamako, and oust the democratically elected president.

Soon after, the Tuareg rebels were muscled aside by heavily-armed Islamist rebels who began taking over the country. This, in turn, prompted the United States to back a 2013 invasion by French and African forces which arrested the complete collapse of Mali — leaving it in a permanent state of occupation and low-level insurgency. Meanwhile, Islamist fighters and Gaddafi's weapons were scattered across Africa, contributing to greater instability in Nigeria and Libya, as well as increased threat levels in Chad, Burkina Faso, Ghana, Guinea, Niger, Senegal, and Togo. It evidently also spurred an audacious revenge attack in Algeria that left more than 80 dead and an assault on a French-run uranium mine and a nearby military base in Niger in which at least 25 people were killed.

TWO SYSTEMS, ONE CONTINENT

In 2000, a report prepared under the auspices of the U.S. Army War College's Strategic Studies Institute examined the "African security environment." While it touched on "internal separatist or rebel movements" in "weak states," as well as non-state actors like militias and "warlord armies," there is conspicuously no mention of Islamic extremism or major transnational terrorist threats.

Following the 9/11 attacks, a senior Pentagon official claimed that the U.S. invasion of Afghanistan might drive "terrorists" out of that country and into African nations, but when pressed about actual transnational dangers on that continent, he admitted that even hard-core Somali militants "really have not engaged in acts of terrorism outside Somalia."

Despite this, Washington dispatched personnel to Africa in 2002 and began pouring money into counterter-rorism efforts. Since then, the United States has steadily increased its military footprint, its troop levels, and its missions on the continent — from night raids in Somalia and kidnap operations in Libya to the construction of a string of bases devoted to surveillance activities across the northern tier of Africa.

For all the time spent training proxies, all the propa-ganda efforts, all the black ops missions, all the counter-terror funds, the results have been dismal. A glance at the official State Department list of terrorist organizations indi-cates that these efforts have been mirrored by the growth of radical militant groups, including the Libyan Islamic Fighting Group added in 2004, al-Shabab in 2008, Ansar al-Dine, Boko Haram, Ansaru, and the al-Mulathamun Battalion in 2013, and Libya's Ansar al-Shari'a in Benghazi, and Ansar al-Shari'a in Darnah, as well as Ansar al-Shari'a in Tunisia, and the Egyptian militant group Ansar Bayt al-Maqdis, all in 2014. And that's hardly a full list. Not included are various terror organizations, rebel forces, separatist movements, armed groups, and militias like the Movement for Unity and Jihad in West Africa, fighters from the group formerly known as Seleka and their rivals, anti-balaka militiamen in the Central African Republic, Taureg separatists of Mali's National Movement for the Liberation of Azawad, the Congolese Resistance Patriots, Burundi's National Forces of Liberation, and others.

Over these years, as the United States has chased terror groups and watched them proliferate, China has taken another route, devoting its efforts to building good-will through public works and winning over governments through "no strings attached" policies.

"Our goal is not to counter China; our goal is not to contain China," President Obama said during a trip to Asia earlier this year. In South Sudan, as in Africa as a whole, the United States seems increasingly unable to even keep up. "On certain levels, we can't or won't compete with China," says the Fund for Peace's Patricia Taft. "China will continue to eclipse us in terms of economic interests in Africa." The United States is, however, still preeminent in the political sphere and that influence, she says, will continue to trump anything China can currently offer.

THE QUESTION IS: FOR HOW LONG?

Cameron Hudson, formerly of the National Security Council and now the acting director of the Center for the Prevention of Genocide at the U.S. Holocaust Museum, thinks strengthening partnerships with the Chinese could lead to major dividends for the United States. "They have more skin in the game," he says of Beijing's relationship with South Sudan. "They have a growing set of interests there."

Benediste Hoareau, head of political affairs for the East African Standby Force — a rapid intervention force in-the-making, consisting of troops from the region's militaries — expresses similar sentiments. He believes in the often repeated axiom of finding African solutions to African problems and says that the foreign powers should provide the funds and let African forces do the fighting and peacekeeping in South Sudan.

Hoareau, in fact, sees no need for a contest, new Cold War or otherwise, between the foreign titans here. There are plenty of opportunities for both the United States and China in Africa and in South Sudan, he tells TomDispatch. A rivalry between the two powers can only bring trouble. "They're elephants," Hoareau says of China and the United States, "and you know just who will g et trampled."

1. What is the relationship between China and Africa?

2. What does China's involvement in Africa tell us about the place of China in regard to the United States and Russia?

"THE COLD WAR NEVER ENDED," BY JOHN FEFFER, FROM *FOREIGN POLICY IN FOCUS*, SEPTEMBER 10, 2014

In '89, it looked as though the war had finally ended.

For five decades the conflict had ground on, and both sides had grown weary of it all. There had been previous pauses in the hostilities, even a détente or two, but this truce looked permanent.

Sure, there were still tensions after '89, and a few skirmishes broke out. But the peace held, miraculously, for more than 25 years. Then, as suddenly as it had begun, the truce collapsed in '15, and the war picked up where it left off.

I'm not predicting the future. I'm talking about 1389.

From 1389 to 1415, the second peace between England and France marked the longest break in the Hundred Years War. But Henry V, who saw no glory in peace, started things up again at the Battle of Agincourt with the cry of "once more unto the breach, my friends!" (or so Shakespeare would have us believe). The conflict would rage for another 40 years until the English were finally kicked back across the Channel for good.

We never know the length of the wars that drag on around us. When peace improbably comes, we'd like to think that the treaties are permanent, that they'll turn former combatants into grumbling but harmless neighbors.

Wars, however, are like acid reflux—they keep recurring no matter how much Pepto-Bismol we chug. Perhaps the Vietnamese thought they'd finally won their independence when they delivered a stinging defeat to the French at Dien Bien Phu in 1954. Perhaps the Afghans imagined that self-determination was theirs when the Soviet superpower withdrew in 1989 (or, for that matter, when the British withdrew in 1880). Wars defy our efforts to write their obituaries.

Indeed, viewed over the long term, war is the very oxygen that we breathe, while peace is but the brief interval when we hold our breath and hope for the best.

The world is currently in the midst of several long wars that don't have any clear endpoint. The battle over the boundaries of the Middle East, set into motion by the disintegration of the Ottoman Empire, continues to rage in Syria, Iraq, and Israel/Palestine. Conflicts over borders inside Africa, ignited by the collapse of colonialism, are still being fought in Congo, Sudan, and elsewhere around the continent. Then there's that great misnomer, the "war on terror," that stretches back before September 11 and will extend well into the future.

By contrast, we've been told ad nauseum that the Cold War is over. I'm sure you remember the funeral. We all watched the corpse lowered into the grave, and we happily lined up to throw a handful of dirt into the hole. The inscription on the gravestone—1946-1991—recorded the conflict's birth in Fulton, Missouri, which was midwifed by Winston Churchill and his infamous Iron Curtain speech, to the quiet death that came with the dissolution of the Soviet Union. But you've seen enough whodunits to suspect, even as you were dancing on the grave, that the coffin buried underneath was empty.

The most obvious evidence that reports of the death of the Cold War had been greatly exaggerated has come from Asia. For two decades, I've had to add parenthetically to my articles on East Asian security that the Cold War may have ended in Europe but it was still alive and well along the Pacific rim. The Communist Parties of China, North Korea, Laos, and Vietnam all refused to follow the example of their European counterparts by stubbornly clinging to the historical stage, by their fingertips if necessary. The Korean peninsula has remained divided between ideologically implacable adversaries, mainland China and the United States continue to regard each other as military competitors, and the region is divided down the middle between China and its allies versus the United States and its allies.

The coffin was empty precisely because the Cold War had lived to fight another day—in the middle of the DMZ, across the Taiwan Strait, among the islands of the South China Sea.

But even in Europe, the traditional narrative of Cold War history has had its irregularities. During the détente period of the 1970s, Washington and Moscow worked out a reasonable modus operandi through arms control treaties, grain sales, and exchanges of ballet troupes. Pundits increasingly subscribed to the convergence theory whereby capitalism became more state-directed and Communism more market-driven. Then came the Soviet invasion of Afghanistan, the victory of Reaganism, the resurgent fear of nuclear war, and it was once more unto the breach, my friends, comrades, and neocons.

In the 1980s, the Soviet leadership became ever more geriatric as Brezhnev, Andropov, and Chernenko passed away in a blur of state funerals. Then it was the Warsaw Pact's time to go into hospice. When Gorbachev stopped supplying Soviet life support, the Soviet bloc expired. Two years later, the Soviet Union followed suit. One side in the global tug-of-war stopped pulling. Game over.

Or maybe not. Maybe everything we've been told about the collapse of the Cold War is false. With the recent conflict in Ukraine, and heightened tensions between Washington and Moscow, observers across the political spectrum speak of a revival of the Cold War—the hawks with anti-Russian relish and the doves with anti-war horror.

But imagine instead that we're in the middle of our own Hundred Years War, and the last 25 years were just a hiatus. After all, many of the features of the Cold War are still in place.

Although two of the Soviet successor states—Ukraine and Kazakhstan—gave up their nuclear weapons, Russia has continued to maintain its much larger arsenal. And the United States has not only barely touched its own equally sizable deterrent force but has thrown billions of dollars into modernizing the very weapons that Obama has pledged to abolish (at some undetermined point in the future). Nor did NATO disappear even though it should have been obvious to everyone—except those on the NATO payroll—that the organization no longer had a purpose. Its vestigial status certainly didn't prevent the alliance from pushing eastward to the very doorstep of Russia's diminished sphere of influence.

The current focus of attention by the Cold War revivalists is the behavior of Vladimir Putin, who has been cast in the role of Henry V. He is responsible for the upsurge in bilateral tensions largely because of his territorial ambitions—first Georgia, then Crimea, and now eastern

Ukraine. He has also played hardball with energy sales to Europe. He continues to back dictators like Assad in Syria. And he has worked to establish geopolitical formations to balance U.S. power—the Eurasian Union with Kazakhstan and Belarus, the Shanghai Cooperation Organization with China and the Central Asian countries, the BRICS with Brazil and India.

Putin's nationalism is noxious, and I've written about the impact of even more intolerant strains of extremism on his policies. But here's the rub: his foreign policies are not substantially different than those pursued by that supposed Westernizer Boris Yeltsin. Russian-backed separatists challenged the sovereignty of the Georgian government in 1992. In that same year, Russian troops also occupied part of Moldova in support of Transnistrian separatists. Hafez al-Assad, Bashar's father, visited Russia in 1999 and Yeltsin proclaimed him "an old friend of Russia." In other words, when it was supposedly under the thrall of liberalism, Russia continued to pursue its interests in the "near abroad" and cultivate controversial allies further afield.

The difference is that Yeltsin did not challenge U.S. unilateral power. Economically weak and no longer able to keep pace with the United States militarily, Russia did not push back hard as NATO expanded eastward, first with its Partnership for Peace and then with actual membership for the former Soviet republics of Estonia, Latvia, and Lithuania. Yeltsin was comfortable being a junior partner of the United States, as long as Washington allowed him latitude in his new circumscribed sphere of influence, permitted

Russia to hold onto its nukes and export cheap jets and tanks, and ushered the country into the G7 and the WTO.

The Cold War, then, was not just about a confrontation between ideological foes. The Cold War was about a confrontation between two countries that each aspired to maintain hegemony over the entire planet. The Soviet Union dropped out of that competition. And Russia under Putin continues to remain focused on concerns along its borders. The United States, on the other hand, has not changed its attitude. And that, ultimately, is why the Cold War never died.

If the United States had disbanded NATO, pushed for nuclear abolition, and helped to create a new security architecture for Europe that included Russia, the Cold War would have died a natural death. Instead, because the institutions of the Cold War lived on, the spirit of the enterprise lay dormant, only waiting for the opportunity to spring forth.

It's not that the United States conjured its Russian adversary back into existence out of some misguided nostalgia. Rather, the inevitable consequence of our refusal to restrain our global ambitions necessarily created a counterforce. In the end, it's boils down to physics: for every action there is an equal and opposite reaction.

So, let's stop talking about the Cold War's revival as if Vladimir Putin is the one who raised the dead. We are the vampire hunters who failed to drive a stake through its heart. So we shouldn't be surprised, when we go out for a stroll one day to survey our domain, to hear the click of sharp teeth poised to tear into its latest victim.

1. To what historical event does the author trace the tension between the United States and Russia? How does he argue that event shapes today's relations?

2. Compare and contrast Russian leaders Boris Yeltsin and Vladimir Putin using examples from the article.

"UKRAINE: THE CLASH OF PARTNERSHIPS," BY JOHN FEFFER, FROM *FOREIGN POLICY IN FOCUS*, MARCH 5, 2014

The Cold War is history. For those growing up today, the Cold War is as distant in time as World War II was for those came of age in the 1970s. In both cases, empires collapsed and maps were redrawn. Repugnant ideologies were laid bare and then laid to rest, though patches of nostalgia persist.

Surely the Cold War has been consigned to the textbooks as irrevocably as the Battle of the Bulge. The Berlin Wall is in pieces. The U.S. president speaks of the abolition of nuclear weapons. The "common European home" from the Atlantic to the Urals—a conceit embraced by such odd bedfellows as De Gaulle and Gorbachev—beckons on the horizon, with the OSCE in place and the European Union creeping ever eastward. Tensions inevitably crop up, but they're nothing worth exchanging ICBMs over.

What was once confrontation has turned into joint efforts to address global challenges: stabilizing the world economy, negotiating nuclear agreements with Iran, ending the war in Syria. A long article in *The New Yorker* on a multi-billion dollar nuclear fusion project being constructed in France reminds us that this quest for a sustainable replacement for fossil fuels began as a late Cold War agreement between Moscow and Washington. Impending environmental catastrophe is gradually uniting all sides in much the same way that Ronald Reagan once imagined that a Martian invasion would.

And then there's Ukraine.

Just when you thought it was safe to get back into geopolitics, the Cold War has reared its ugly head once again. All your favorite characters have returned to the footlights—the iron-fisted Russian leader, the thundering American secretary of state, troops of multiple nations on alert, and lots of cloak-and-dagger intrigue behind the scenes. And starring in the role of Prague 1968 is that new and untested actor: Crimea 2014. We can only hope that history is repeating itself as farce, not as a tragic tale told twice.

But there are some crucial differences in this restaging of the Cold War classic. The West has not been practicing containment of Russia so much as rollback of its influence by expanding NATO and the EU up to the country's doorstep. And Moscow is not invoking some form of internationalism in support of ideological compatriots but nationalism pure and simple to safeguard its ethnic brethren. Moreover, this is a democratic age: Russian military intervention now comes with the Duma's imprimatur. From the West, so far, has come much sound and fury, including the threat of economic sanctions and other penalties, but a military response remains off the table. There is still time to find a diplomatic solution that can preserve Ukrainian sovereignty, address the concerns of Russians on both sides of the border, and revive that old vision of a common European home that treats Russia as a member, not a mobster.

When people speak of "Russia's doorstep," they mean Ukraine. No one aspires to be a doorstep, because that's what people walk on with their muddy boots. As Timothy Snyder has detailed in his book Bloodlands, Ukraine has suffered incalculable losses because of its location, first as a locus of potential resistance to Soviet control and then as a battleground during World War II. War pushed the country's boundaries westward to incorporate what had once been parts of Poland. Changing the map only further emphasized Ukraine's centrality to the fate of Europe, particularly after the disintegration of the Soviet Union in 1991. The western sections have leaned Europe-ward while large numbers of Russian speakers in the east feel some measure of allegiance to Moscow.

It's not just language that pulls Ukraine in two directions like the poor baby in King Solomon's parable. It's also a question of which collective entity to huddle in for shelter. Ukraine joined Russia and Belarus to create the Commonwealth of Independent States (CIS) in December 1991 as the Soviet Union fell to pieces around them. But Ukraine was also the first CIS member to join NATO's Partnership for Peace program in 1994. Fifteen years later, Ukraine signed up for the European Union's Eastern Partnership. Russia has not been happy about either of these partnerships. Moscow put together its own partnership, the Eurasian

Economic Community, more than a dozen years ago, but Ukraine is only an observer.

A clash of partnerships is now threatening to break out on the peninsula of Crimea. This semi-autonomous region is the only part of Ukraine with a majority of Russian speakers, and it also hosts Russia's Black Sea fleet. In Crimea's 2010 parliamentary elections, Viktor Yanukovych's Russophone Party of Regions scored a huge victory. But a large population of Crimean Tatars—15 percent of the 2 million people who live on the peninsula—has rallied in support of the new government in Kiev. The sympathies of Crimeans are clearly divided.

And now, it seems, Crimea itself is divided. Armed men stormed the Crimean parliament last week and forced the appointment of Sergei Aksyonov as the new prime minister of the peninsula. Aksyonov immediately appealed to Russia for assistance and set a date for a referendum on Crimean independence. Russian troops have spread throughout the peninsula to secure both civilian and military installations. Russian guards are posted outside Ukrainian military bases. The peninsula is divided between pro-Russian and pro-Ukrainian forces, with Aksyonov already declaring a new Crimean army that he insists Ukrainian soldiers must join.

Russian troops conducting exercises at the border recently returned home, and Vladimir Putin has said that his country has no intention of swallowing Crimea. Indeed, absorption might not be his goal, for even the tastiest morsels have a habit of sticking in the throat.

Crimea is not the only challenge to Ukraine's unity. Kharkiv, located a scant 40 kilometers from the border with Russia, is the country's second largest city.

Earlier in the week, a group of Cossacks seized control of the city hall and hoisted a Russian flag. But the new Ukrainian authorities eventually reestablished control. Places like Crimea and Kharkiv could swing either way in their sympathies. Russian troops plus separatist sentiment could produce an Abkhazian or Transnistrian scenario: breakaway provinces recognized by only a handful of countries around the world. Only compromise—a free-and-fair referendum, the preservation of minority rights, a moratorium on NATO expansion—can prevent fracture.

The continuing crisis in Ukraine has generated its share of Cold War-style inanities. One favorite trope of that period was the "mote in your eye" accusation. Secretary of State John Kerry, who apparently only lives in the present, recently intoned that "you just don't invade another country on phony pretexts in order to assert your interests." Then there's the "if they only had nukes" argument. John Mearsheimer thinks Ukraine shouldn't have given up its nuclear arsenal back in 1994 because those weapons would have made Russia think twice about sending troops into Crimea. Will the MAD scientists never learn? The situation in Ukraine is bad enough without adding WMD to the mix whether in the form of deliberate attack, accidental use, or loose nukes.

But the chief inanity is the one that has governed Western policy since 1991—that there would be no costs to the expansion of NATO and the European Union. Leaders in Washington and Brussels have been repeatedly warned by those with even just a passing familiarity with Russian history and culture that encroachment in Moscow's sphere of influence—its "near abroad"—is tantamount to poking the bear. Yes, it's true that both institutions are responding to genuine interest "on the ground." But the stakes here are very high. It's not just about "losing Ukraine." It would be an even greater catastrophe to "lose Russia." And here I mean not the Cold War game of winning and losing but the more universal struggle between a liberating order and a debilitating chaos.

Indeed, with the rise of Putin and the freeze that has settled over freedom of expression and assembly, Russia is already being lost by degrees. It can't be allowed to drift further into the politics of reaction. But the traditional approach to "saving Russia" has been a dual strategy of rolling back its influence externally and funding democracy initiatives within the country.

However much I would love to see Ukraine in the European Union one day and however much I support civil society initiatives inside Russia, enthusiasts for these projects must recognize that they strengthen the hands of those who argue the West is only interested in neutering Mother Russia. Backlash is almost inevitable.

Policymakers in Washington and Brussels should take a much longer view. Instead of concentrating on "partnerships" that put Russia beyond the pale, they have to revive a much more encompassing vision of European security. As long as we continue to shave away at the habitat where the bear lives, it will swipe at its encroachers and defend its ground. "Some days you'll eat the bear," goes the old Joan Armatrading song, while "some days the bear will eat you."

It might seem ridiculous to talk about grand partnerships with Russia at the very moment when the international community wants to put Putin in the penalty box. But Russia is much bigger than just Vladimir Putin, despite the man's penchant for self-aggrandizement. Making a place at the table for this vast country is a chief challenge for the 21st century. So, even as we condemn the introduction of Russian troops in Crimea and decry the narrowing of democratic freedoms in Moscow, we have to remember that the Cold War is over, it should never return, and both sides must act that way.

1. Why does the author feel the Cold War would play out differently today than it did in the past?

2. What is Ukraine's relationship with the EU and how does that shape its place between the United States and Russia?

CHAPTER 6

WHAT ORDINARY PEOPLE SAY

The Cold War was a conflict that played out at the highest levels of political, military, and cultural power. But the people impacted were ordinary citizens of both the United States and the Soviet Union, as well as countries around the world that became caught up in the rivalry. Whether it was fear of nuclear fallout or repression due to Soviet crackdowns, Americans and Soviets alike lived in a state of uncertainty, which shaped anxieties and cast a long shadow into our modern lives. A new Cold War would do the same, and many citizens have voiced concern about what a similar conflict would mean for the world today. By drawing on their experiences during the Cold War and scholarship on the conflict that has been written since, their accounts are a sobering reminder of the human cost of international rivalry.

"6 REASONS NOT TO REBOOT THE COLD WAR," BY MIRIAM PEMBERTON, FROM *OTHERWORDS*, FEBRUARY 9, 2016

The Pentagon budget unveiled this week calls for quadrupling spending on efforts to counter Russia. The money would move more troops, tanks, and artillery into position near the Russia border. This last Obama budget would also fund another installment in a $1 trillion and 30-year plan to "modernize" our nuclear arsenal with new land-based missiles, bombers and submarines.

If Congress supports the White House's request, this budget would have our country spending more, adjusting for inflation, than we did during most of the Cold War. The Republican-controlled Congress wants to add even more. Sounds like we're gearing up for a reboot of that war, doesn't it? Here are six reasons why this is a big mistake.

1. It's what Putin wants.

As the Russian economy squeezes the lives of Russian citizens ever tighter, Putin is doing what Russia's strongmen leaders have always done: Distract them with dreams of a return to their imperial past. Appeal to their centuries-old sense of insecurity about external threats, whose only cure is militarism. What plays into this narrative best? The U.S. and NATO amassing troops on their border.

2. It's what Pentagon contractors want.

Twenty-five years after the Soviet empire collapsed, the U.S. military remains built for confrontations with "great powers." As the Pentagon conceives it, the fight against ISIS is relatively cheap, and requires flexibility that doesn't fit well with the nice long procurement cycles the contractors favor. ISIS has no fighter jets, a fact that complicates the sales pitch for the $1.5 trillion dollar F-35 fighter jet program. A new Cold War would make that job a lot easier.

3. Contrary to popular belief, the Reagan military build-up didn't bring the Soviet Union to its knees.

The idea that it did is one of the big myths of the late 20th century. It's refuted by the guy who would actually know: the last Soviet leader, who presided over its military stand-down. Mikhail Gorbachev has said repeatedly in retirement that the buildup made it harder to convince his hardliners that they didn't need to respond in kind, but could negotiate reductions in the nuclear arsenal. It prolonged, rather than ended, the Cold War.

4. We can't afford it.

We're now spending more than the next 13 countries put together, and more than three times as much as

China. Nine times as much as Russia. Meanwhile the water crisis in Flint, Michigan points to the consequences of our neglect of our country's infrastructure. According to the National Priorities Project, foregoing the cost of beefing up our nuclear arsenal for one year would enable U.S. to send nearly 600,000 more students to college for four years. Instead we want to spend more to rekindle the Cold War?

5. It'll undermine the most significant diplomatic success in recent years.
The international agreement preventing Iran from building a nuclear weapon for years to come would not have been possible without Russia's support. It was one of the rare bright spots in U.S.-Russian relations. Something to build on. Putting troops and artillery back on the Russian border will threaten this tenuous progress.

6. It could trigger a nuclear holocaust.
Following the end of the (what we may soon have to call the first) Cold War, the United States and Russia negotiated steep cuts in each country's nuclear arsenal, though there are still enough on both sides to destroy the world many times over. As signatories to the Nuclear Nonproliferation Treaty, they committed to getting to zero. They also cooperated for years on securing stockpiles of nuclear materials around the world to keep them out of terrorist hands. That progress is now stalled, as Washington pursues its

"modernization." No other fact threatens our very existence the way this one does. Do we really want to return to the days when these weapons were on hair-trigger alert, and the countries possessing them considered themselves at war? President Barack Obama, who won the Nobel Peace Prize on the strength of his commitment to nuclear disarmament, should know better.

1. Based on the readings in this collection, do you agree with the author's arguments about why a new Cold War would be negative?

2. Choose one of the six items in this article. Can you find any arguments against it?

EXCERPT FROM "NINA TURNER: WHILE CONGRESS OBSESSES OVER RUSSIA, AMERICANS BEING 'LEFT BEHIND," BY LAUREN MCCAULEY, FROM *COMMON DREAMS*, MAY 29, 2017

Former Ohio state Sen. Nina Turner is worried that Americans are being "left behind" because Congress and the media are seemingly consumed by "Russia, Russia, Russia."

During a panel discussion on *CNN's* "State of the Union" on Sunday, Turner was asked about the latest revelations that President Donald Trump's son-in-law Jared Kushner had attempted to establish "back channels" of communication with the Kremlin.

"How's this playing in Ohio?" asked guest host Dana Bash.

Turner responded: "No one in Ohio is asking about Russia."

"I mean, we have to deal with this," she continued, referring to the ongoing investigation into alleged election meddling. "We definitely have to deal with this. It's on the minds of the American people. But you want to know about people in Ohio—they want to know about jobs. They want to know about their children."

Turner, a vocal supporter of Sen. Bernie Sanders (I-Vt.) during his presidential campaign, said she has spoken with voters across the country and found widespread concern over domestic issues and feelings that they are not being represented by the dominant political class.

She said she was just in California where folks are currently pushing for a single-payer healthcare program. She said she also recently "talked to an African American baby boomer" living in Washington, D.C.. "Russia is not in his top five [concerns]," she said. "He thinks both parties are failing."

"I talked to a Gen Xer white male who is in the union," who she said would rather vote for a third party. "We are losing," said Turner, of the Democratic Party establishment.

"The president should be concerned about this, all Americans should be concerned about this," she said, but added that "should we go to Flint, [Michigan] they wouldn't ask you about Russia and Jared Kushner. They want to know how they are gonna get some clean water and why some 8,000 people are about to lose their homes.

"We are preoccupied with this," Turner added, "it's not that this is not important, but every day Americans are being left behind because it's Russia, Russia, Russia. Do we need all 535 members of Congress to deal with Russia? Can some of them deal with some domestic issues?"

The remarks come as Republican senators are working to put together their version of the House healthcare bill, which the Congressional Budget Office estimates would strip health insurance from 23 million people. Congress is also poised to begin debating Trump's budget, unveiled last week, which takes an axe to domestic spending, including essential social safety nets.

Turner is not the first to suggest that Congressional Democrats are jumping on the Russia controversy to avoid supporting populist economic solutions, such as Medicare-for-All.

As journalist David Sirota noted on Twitter Sunday:

"Theory: Dems love Russiagate because it lets them both slam Trump & avoid promoting a populist economic message their donors hate […] This doesn't mean Russia-Trump stuff isn't really important – it is. But it explains (in part) why it is crowding everything else out."

He added: "'You'll have to wait till after the Russia probe for us to address millions not being able to afford healthcare' may not be a great message."

1. Do you agree with the author's assertion that there might be more secretive political reasons for certain politicians to clamor for media attention on Russia's influence in the 2016 presidential elections?

"IS PUTIN'S RUSSIA THE CRITICAL THREAT AMERICANS BELIEVE IT TO BE?," BY RONALD SUNY, FROM *THE CONVERSATION*, JUNE 26, 2017

At least four U.S. intelligence agencies agree that evidence shows the Russian government hacked the Democratic National Committee and waged a campaign to influence voters in 2016.Although no evidence of collusion between U.S. citizens and Russia has been proven yet, President Donald Trump and Secretary of State Rex Tillerson's attempt to improve relations with Russia has been hobbled.

The cloud hanging over the White House seems to be growing, with Congress considering sanctions against Russia. A majority of Americans view Russia unfavorably and believe it represents a threat, according to Gallup. Russia is depicted daily as a major menace to the United States. The slightest concession by an American to a Russian overture has become suspicious and smells of capitulation.

As a historian who has watched and written about the rocky ride Russians have experienced since the collapse of the USSR, I offer a look at the broader context of U.S.-Russia relations.

While Russia has certainly caused mischief for Washington and Europe, I don't believe we should consider negotiation and compromise with Putin as appeasement – as we did during the Cold War. Careful consideration of how Russia views its own vital interests may help us see past the noise.

HOW BIG A THREAT IS RUSSIA?

In reality, the most powerful country in history and on the globe at the moment, the United States, faces a considerably weaker adversary in Russia.

The Kremlin spends about 10 percent of what the United States spendson defense (US$600 billion). The United States spends more on defense than the next eight countries combined.

Putin slashed military spending a few months ago by 25.5 percent, just as Trump plans to increase American defense spending by more than $54 billion.

Russia's economy pales in comparison to America, Europe, Japan and China. It has an economy roughly the size of Italy's, but must provide for a larger population, territory and defense budget.

It's true that a somewhat weaker power can annoy, pressure or even harm a stronger power. And while Russia has a huge nuclear arsenal and impressive cyber capabilities, it is seriously outmatched by the United States in terms of influence and power. Obama referred to Russia as "a regional power," and Putin thinks of America as a "global hegemon." There are important truths in both of their statements.

Both Putin and his predecessor, the late Russian President Boris Yeltsin, repeatedly complained about the expansion of NATO into Eastern Europe, and even into countries formerly part of the Soviet Union – the Baltic republics of Estonia, Latvia and Lithuania. The Kremlin made its opposition clear in 2008 when it launched a devastating incursion into Georgia, a country that hoped to join NATO. In 2014, Russia, Europe and the United States maneuvered for dominance in Ukraine – this time Russia lost. Moscow exacted its revenge by annexing Crimea in March 2014, which only drove Ukraine deeper into the arms of the West.

Putin occasionally overreaches, as he did in Crimea. Yet the Russian president usually plays his comparatively weak hand rather shrewdly. In Syria, for example, Putin supports the Bashar al-Assad government, a truly vicious regime that is prepared to kill hundreds of thousands of its citizens to hold on to power. Here the United States tried regime change, but Putin and Iran's backing of Damascus made that impossible. As both the Obama and Trump administrations struggled to formulate a policy in Syria, Putin effectively marginalized the United States by forging a common front with Turkey and Iran.

And while the United States and Russia might disagree about the Syrian regime, they do have some common ground. Both powers have decided that the first priority is to combat the Islamic State. Both countries have found reliable allies against IS in the Syrian Kurds, which my research suggests is a distinct nation prepared to fight for their autonomy or independence. Despite

Russia's first priority to defend Assad's government, both the United States and Russia appear at the moment to be working together with the Syrian Kurds to contain IS, the most immediate danger to the Middle East and by extension much of the world.

The crises over Syria, Ukraine and Georgia, as well as Russia's blustering threats against the Baltic republics, all are responses of a relatively vulnerable, less-than-superpower. Russians feel threatened, humiliated by the West's military expansion eastward. American troops regularly exercise in what was once the Soviet Bloc. American rockets have been placed in the Czech Republic and Poland. Russian and American planes buzz each other near the Russian enclave of Kaliningrad.

Although it is unable to reestablish the kind of dominance in Eastern Europe that it enjoyed during the Cold War, the Kremlin is determined to retain an influential position in the part of the world closest to its borders. What we are watching, in my view, is an uneven struggle between a real superpower and global hegemon, the United States, and a regional hegemon, Russia, that feels it has been backed into a corner.

COMMON INTERESTS

More than anything else, in my opinion, Russians wish to be taken seriously.

Putin still refers to the United States not as an adversary but as a partner, as he did repeatedly in interviews with film director Oliver Stone. At the same time, unwilling to accept American global dominance without challenge, he fails to face the effects his policies have on Western leaders and the broader public. He repeatedly declares he is perplexed by the hysteria in America that demonizes Russia.

While investigations into Russian hacking and Trump's campaign ties must continue, the major hot spots mentioned above will continue to smolder and may suddenly flare up. The stakes are high and Russian and American interests coincide in many areas. There are few that can not be ameliorated, if not fully resolved, through negotiation.

Yet, the distance between the two countries grows wider by the day. Wrangling inside the Beltway – one of the signs of a healthy democracy – continues. But above the din, few voices can be heard calling for a more sober and farsighted evaluation of our strategic interests. In my years as a historian, I have found that it is precisely in such moments of heightened confrontation and deafness to the interests of others that unpredictable and destructive conflicts break out. As impossible as it seems at the moment to deescalate inflammatory rhetoric, I believe only discussion and negotiation offer a way forward.

CONCLUSION

The Cold War was a complex conflict that lasted for decades, touching the lives of people around the world. Although it ended formally in 1991, some experts feel the tension between the United States and Russia has lingered through today, shaping the relationship between the two countries. That tension has increased in recent years, leading many to suggest we are entering a period that could be called a new Cold War, or a period of rivalry that has potential to threaten the world order.

As we have seen in the articles in this book, the question of the conflict between the United States and Russia is historically and politically complex. While Russia's increased drive to gain influence around the world has made many uneasy, the United States has responded harshly— driving potential conflict in a way that some believe is not in our national interest. Propaganda, social media, and competing messages between the two countries have all played a role in creating an atmosphere of rivalry and ill-will, which could boil over into more direct conflict if unchecked.

Although the way forward is unclear and relations remain tense between the two countries, it is important to remember that the world is much different today than it was when the Cold War was at its height in the latter half of the twentieth century. Today, China is a rising power with the clout to upend the system that has allowed Russia and the United States to sit as the two poles of world power for many decades. China, an economic and military power in its own right, poses a unique challenge and opportunity—and could emerge as a rival to both Russia and the United States as the country expands its influence.

A new Cold War is far from guaranteed. But as we move toward conflict, it is important to learn from the past and look to the future as a means to secure lasting and effective peace.

BIBLIOGRAPHY

Bice, Allie. "McCain Warns Against Russian Overtures, a Day After Trump, Putin Talk." *Cronkite News*, November 15, 2016. https://cronkitenews.azpbs.org/2016/11/15/mccain-warns-against-russian-overtures-one-day-after-trump-putin-talk.

Cheskin, Ammon. "Ukraine, Kremlin Propaganda and the Cold War Trap." *The Conversation*, March 25, 2014. https://theconversation.com/ukraine-kremlin-propaganda-and-the-cold-war-trap-24745.

Cilluffo, Frank J. "Russia's Aggressive Power is Resurgent, Online and Off." *The Conversation*, August 26, 2016. https://theconversation.com/russias-aggressive-power-is-resurgent-online-and-off-64336.

Ciolan, Ionela Maria. "The Role of the 'New Cold War' Concept in Constructing Russia's Great Power Narrative." *CES Working Papers*, Volume VIII, Issue 4. http://www.ceswp.uaic.ro/articles/CESWP2016_VIII4_CIO.pdf.

Conley, Julie. "Tensions Rise as Russia Retaliates Against New Sanctions Bill." *Common Dreams*, July 28, 2017. https://www.commondreams.org/news/2017/07/28/tensions-rise-russia-retaliates-against-new-sanctions-bill.

Feffer, John. "The Cold War Never Ended." *Foreign Policy in Focus*, September 10. 2014. http://fpif.org/cold-war-never-ended.

Feffer, John. "Ukraine: The Clash of Partnerships." *Foreign Policy in Focus*, March 5, 2014. http://fpif.org/ukraine-clash-partnerships.

Felle, Tom. "Facebook's 'Fake News' Plan is Doomed to Failure - Social Media Must Do More to Counter Disinformation." *The Conversation*, April 11, 2017. https://theconversation.com/facebooks-fake-news-plan-is-doomed-to-failure-social-media-must-do-more-to-counter-disinformation-75953.

Hooper, Cynthia. "Russia Fighting Information Wars with Borrowed Weapons." *The Conversation*, March 30, 2015. https://theconversation.com/russia-fighting-information-wars-with-borrowed-weapons-37960.

Hunter, Brittany. "No Good Can Come From Trying to Resurrect the Cold War." *Foundation for Economic Education*, May 29, 2017. https://fee.org/articles/no-good-can-come-from-trying-to-resurrect-the-cold-war.

Marshall, Rachelle. "US Needs to Think Twice Before Reprising the Cold War." *Foreign Policy in Focus*, February 9, 2016. http://fpif.org/u-s-needs-think-twice-reprising-cold-war.

McCauley, Lauren. "Nina Turner: While Congress Obsesses Over Russia, Americans Being 'Left Behind'." *Common Dreams*, May

29, 2017. https://www.commondreams.org/news/2017/05/29
/nina-turner-while-congress-obsesses-over-russia-americans
-being-left-behind.

McClennen, Sophia A. "Can a Russian-Funded Cable Network
Actually Promote Free Press in the US?" *The Conversation*,
March 29, 2016. https://theconversation.com/can-a-russian
-funded-cable-network-actually-promote-free-press-in-the
-u-s-54620.

Moir, Matt. "What's Fueling China's Aggressive Crackdown on
Activism and Media?" *Waging Non-Violence*, Mary 12, 2016.
https://wagingnonviolence.org/feature/whats-fueling-chi-
nas-aggressive-crackdown-on-activism-and-media.

Pemberton, Miriam. "6 Reasons Not to Reboot the Cold War."
Other Words, February 9, 2016. http://otherwords.org/6-reasons
-not-to-reboot-the-cold-war.

Price, Ned. "The Administration's Response to Russia: What You
Need To Know." *The White House Archives*, December 29, 2016.
https://obamawhitehouse.archives.gov/blog/2016/12/29/presi-
dents-response-russias-actions-during-2016-election-what
-you-need-know.

Reynolds, David and Kristina Spohr. "Opinion: Thirty years On as
'New Cold War' Looms, US and Russia Should Remember the
Rekyjavik Summit." *The Conversation*, October 19, 2016.
https://theconversation.com/thirty-years-on-as-new-cold-war-
looms-us-and-russia-should-remember-the-reykjavik
-summit-67084.

Rotella, Sebastian. "Russia's Shadow-War in a Wary Europe."
Propublica, April 4, 2017. https://www.propublica.org/article
/russias-shadow-war-in-a-wary-europe.

Sigal, Ivan. "Fake News and Fake Solutions: How Do We Build A
Civics of Trust?" *Global Voices*, March 20, 2017. https://advox
.globalvoices.org/2017/03/20/fake-news-and-fake-solutions
-how-do-we-build-a-civics-of-trust.

Slaveski, Filip. "Are Europe and the World Slipping Back into
a Second Cold War?" *The Conversation*, November 18, 2014.
https://theconversation.com/are-europe-and-the-world-slip-
ping-back-into-a-second-cold-war-34017.

Staff. "Remarks by the Vice President and Georgian Prime Minister in a Joint Press Conference." *The White House*, August 1,
2017. https://www.whitehouse.gov/the-press-office/2017/08/01
/remarks-vice-president-and-georgian-prime-minister
-joint-press.

Staff. "Statement by the President on Actions in Response to Russian Malicious Cyber Activity and Harassment." *The White House Archives*, December 29, 2016.

Staff. "Statement by the President on New Sanctions Related to Russia." *The White House Archives*, September 11, 2014. https://obamawhitehouse.archives.gov/the-press-office/2016/12/29/statement-president-actions-response-russian-malicious-cyber-activity.

Staff. "Vice President Biden's Remarks at Moscow State University." *The White House Archives*, March 10, 2011. https://obamawhitehouse.archives.gov/the-press-office/2011/03/10/vice-president-bidens-remarks-moscow-state-university.

Stevens, Tim. "Cyber Espionage and the New Cold War of US-China Relations." *The Conversation*, May 21, 2014. https://theconversation.com/cyber-espionage-and-the-new-cold-war-of-us-china-relations-26975.

Suny, Ronald. "Is Putin's Russia the Critical Threat Americans Believe It to Be?" *The Conversation*, June 26, 2017. https://theconversation.com/is-putins-russia-the-critical-threat-americans-believe-it-to-be-77531.

Thornton, Gabriela Marin and Alexey Ilin. "The Real Winner of the Ukraine Crisis Could Be China." *The Conversation*, February 23, 2015. https://theconversation.com/the-real-winner-of-the-ukraine-crisis-could-be-china-37574.

Tucker, Jeffrey A. "The Russia Sanctions Are About Controlling Americans." *Foundation for Economic Education*, July 25, 2017. https://fee.org/articles/the-russia-sanctions-are-about-controlling-americans.

Turse, Nick. "China, America, and a New Cold War in Africa?" *Foreign Policy in Focus*, August 5, 2014. http://fpif.org/china-america-new-cold-war-africa.

Vladimirova, Anastasia. "Debunking Russia's Fake Popular Struggle in Ukraine." *Waging Non-Violence*, October 13, 2015. https://wagingnonviolence.org/feature/debunking-russias-fake-popular-struggle-ukraine.

CHAPTER NOTES

CHAPTER 1: WHAT THE EXPERTS SAY

EXCERPT FROM "THE ROLE OF THE 'NEW COLD WAR' CONCEPT IN CONSTRUCTING RUSSIA'S GREAT POWER NARRATIVE"
BY IONELA MARIA CIOLAN

1. As was demonstrated by the research conducted by Political Capital Institute entitled "The Russian connection, the spread of pro-Russian policies on the European far right", published on 14th March 2014 and available at: http://pdc.ceu.hu /archive/00007035/01/PC_Russian-Connection_2014.pdf, last accessed on 21st August 2016.

2. These alleged Russian cyber-acts are still under investigation. Source: http://www.reuters.com/article/us-usa-cyberme-dia-idUSKCN10Y21I, last accessed on 23th August 2016.

3. More on this subject: "Russia Accuses Kyiv Of Plotting 'Terror' In Crimea; Ukraine Denounces Moscow's 'Fantasies'", in Radio Free Europe, published on 10th August 2016 and available at: http://www.rferl.org/a/crimea-fsb-ukraineincursion/27912985. html, last accessed on 11th August 2016.

REFERENCES

Allison, R. (2014), "Russian 'deniable' intervention in Ukraine: how and why Russia broke the rules", *International Affairs*, Vol. 90, No. 6.

Arbatov, A. (2007), "Is a new Cold War imminent?", *Russia in Global Affairs*, August 8, available at: http://eng.globalaffairs.ru/number/n_9127 (accessed September 17, 2016).

Baker, P., Erlanger, S. (2015), "Russia Uses Money and Ideology to Fight Western Sanctions", *The New York Times*, June 7, available at: http://www.nytimes.com/2015/06/08/world/Europe /russia-fights-wests-ukraine-sanctions-with-aid-and-ideology.html (accessed September 15, 2016).

Baylis, J., Smith, S. and Owens, P. (2011), *The Globalization of World Politics, An introduction to international relations*, 5th Edition, Oxford University Press, New York.

BBC (2014), "How far do EU-US sanctions on Russia go?", September 15, available at: http://www.bbc.com/news/world-europe-28400218 (accessed August 15, 2016).

Cohen, S. (2014), *Soviet Fates and Lost Alternatives; From Stalinism to the New Cold War*, Columbia University Press, New York.

Cox, M. (2014), "Learning from history? From Soviet collapse to the 'new' Cold War", *Cold War History*, Vol. 14, No. 4.

Dadak, C. (2010), "A new "Cold War"?", *The Independent Review*, Vol. 15, No. 1.

European Council (2016), "Russia: EU prolongs economic sanctions by six months", December 19, available at: http://www.consilium.europa.eu/en/press/press-releases/2016/12/19-sanctionsrussia/ (accessed December 19, 2016).

Galbreath, D. (2008), "Putin's Russia and the 'New Cold War': Interpreting Myth and Reality", *Europe-Asia Studies*, Vol. 60, No. 9.

Gozman, L. (2016), "Don't Disrespect the Diva: Why Putin's Foreign Policy Is a Quest for Status", *The Moscow Times*, October 7, available at: https://themoscowtimes.com/articles/dontdisrespect-the-diva-why-putins-foreign-policy-is-a-quest-for-status-55657 (accessed November 18, 2016).

Gromyko, A. (2015), "Russia–EU relations at a crossroads: preventing a new Cold War in a polycentric world", *Southeast European and Black Sea Studies*, Vol. 15, No. 2.

Ignatieff, M. (2014), "Is the Age of Intervention Over?", *Chatham House*, March 19, available at:https://www.chathamhouse.org/sites/files/chathamhouse/home/chatham/public_html/sites/default/files/20140319AgeofIntervention.pdf (accessed October 11, 2016).

Itani, F. and Abouzahr, H. (2016), "Lessons from Russia's Interven-tion in Syria", *Atlantic Council*, October 26, available at: http://www.atlanticcouncil.org/blogs/syriasource/lessons-fromrus-sia-s-intervention-in-syria (accessed October 28, 2016).

Legvold, R. (2014), "The New Cold War" , *The Moscow Times*, April 4, available at: https://themoscowtimes.com/articles/the-new-cold-war-33616 (accessed July 18, 2016).

Lukyanov, F. (2011), "The Russian-Georgian war as a turning point", *Russia in Global Affairs*, November 24, available at: http://eng.globalaffairs.ru/redcol/The-Russian-Georgian-war-as-aturning-point-15381 (accessed September 12, 2016).

Lukyanov, F. (2016), "Putin's Foreign Policy", *Russia in Global Affairs*, May 9, available at: http://eng.globalaffairs.ru/redcol/Putins-Foreign-Policy-18133 (accessed July 28, 2016).

M. Hudson, V. (2005), "Foreign Policy Analysis: Actor-Specific The-ory and the Ground of International Relations", *Foreign Policy Analysis*, Vol. 1.

McEldowney, J. (2016), "The Russian ban on agricultural prod-ucts", *European Parliament Research Service*, April, available at: http://www.europarl.europa.eu/RegData/etudes/BRIE/2016/581971/EPRS_BRI(2016)581971_EN.pdf (accessed August 2016, 21).

Medvedev, D. (2009), "Presidential Address to the Federal Assem-bly of the Russian Federation", President of Russia, November 12, available at: http://en.special.kremlin.ru/ events/president/transcripts/5979 (accessed August 8, 2016).

Menkiszak, M. (2015/2016), *Russia's long war on Ukraine*, Paper Series, no.1, Transatlantic Academy.

Meyer, H., Wishart, I., and Biryukov, A. (2015), "Russia's Medvedev: We Are in 'a New Cold War'", Bloomberg, February 13, avail-able at: http://www.bloomberg.com/news/articles/2016- 02-13/russia-sees-new-cold-war-as-nato-chief-criticizes-nuclear-threat (accessed August 3, 2016).

NATO (2016a), "NATO-Russia Council", April 15, available at: http://www.nato.int/ cps/en/natohq/topics_50091.htm (accessed August 7, 2016).

NATO (2016b), "Doorstep statement by NATO Secretary General Jens Stoltenberg", July 8, available at: http://www.nato.int/cps /en/natohq/opinions_133260.htm (accessed July 29, 2016).

Oliphant, R. (2016), "Russia and the West have 'entered a new Cold War'", *The Telegraph*. October 23, available at: http://www .telegraph.co.uk/news/2016/10/22/unyielding-russia-and-ush-eading-for-a-new-cold-war/ (accessed October 25, 2016).

Omelicheva, M., Zubytska, L. (2016), "An Unending Quest for Russia's Place in the World: The Discursive Co-evolution of the Study and Practice of International Relations in Russia", *New Perspectives, Interdisciplinary Journal of Central & East European Politics and International Relations*, Vol. 24, No. 1.

Parket, L. (2016), "JIT: Flight MH17 was shot down by a BUK missile from a farmland near Pervomaiskyi", *Openbaar Ministerie*, September 26, available at: Ionela Maria CIOLAN 645 https:// www.om.nl/onderwerpen/mh17-crash/@96068/jit-flight-mh17-shot/ (accessed September 27, 2016).

Political Capital Institute (2014), "The Russian connection, the spread of pro-Russian policies on the European far right", March 14, available at: http://pdc.ceu.hu/archive/00007035/ 01 /PC_Russian-Connection_2014.pdf (accessed August 21, 2016).

Putin, V. (2007a), "Putin's Prepared Remarks at 43rd Munich Conference on Security Policy," *The Washington Post*, February 12, available at: http://www.washingtonpost.com/wpdyn/content /article/2007/02/12/AR2007021200555.html (accessed August 1, 2016).

Putin, V. (2007b), "Speech at the Military Parade Celebrating the 62nd Anniversary of Victory in the Great Patriotic War", May 9, available at: http://en.kremlin.ru/events/president/ tran-scripts/24238 (accessed July 21, 2016).

Putin, V. (2014), "Address by President of the Russian Federation", President of Russia, March 18, available at: http://en.kremlin. ru/events/president/news/20603 (accessed September 16, 2016).

Radio Free Europe (2016), "Russia Accuses Kyiv Of Plotting 'Terror' In Crimea; Ukraine Denounces Moscow's 'Fantasies'", August 10, available at: http://www.rferl.org/content/crimea-fs-bukraine-incursion/27912985.html (accessed August 11, 2016).

Reuters (2016), "New York Times says suspected Russian hackers targeted Moscow bureau", August 23, available at: http://www.reuters.com/article/us-usa-cyber-media-idUSKCN10Y21I (accessed August 23, 2016).

Rotaru, V. (2014), *The Eastern Partnership, A Turning Point in EU-Russia Relations?*, Military Publishing House, Bucharest.

Rumer, E. (2016), "The Kremlin's Advantage", *Foreign Affairs*, August 2, available at: https://www.foreignaffairs.com/articles /russian-federation/2016-08-02/kremlins-advantage (accessed August 7, 2016).

Russia Today (2015), "West fears recreation of Soviet Union, despite nobody planning one – Putin", December 21, available at: https://www.rt.com/news/326666-putin-ukraine-soviet-unionturkey/ (accessed November 23, 2016).

Russia Today (2016a), "World would be more balanced if Russia asserted national interests from outset – Putin", January 11, available at: https://www.rt.com/news/328473-world-balance-russian-interests-putin/ (accessed November 13, 2016).

Russia Today (2016b), "NATO used Ukraine conflict to overcome 'identity crisis' – Russian envoy", February 23, available at: https://www.rt.com/news/333310-nato-russia-ukraine-crisis / (accessed December 1, 2016).

Sakwa, R. (2008). "New Cold War" or twenty years' crisis?", *International Affairs*, Vol. 84, No. 2.

Salzman, R. (2014), "Russian Goals for BRICS: Then and Now", *Russian International Affairs Council*, July 24, available at: http://russiancouncil.ru/en/blogs/rachel-salzman/?id_4=1315 (accessed November 13, 2016).

Snyder, T. (2014), "Crimea: Putin vs. Reality", *The New York Review of Books*, March 7, available at: http://www.nybooks.com/ daily/2014/03/07/crimea-putin-vs-reality/ (accessed August 23, 2016).

Speck, U. (2016), "Russia's Challenge to the International Order", *Carnegie Europe*, August 13, available at: http://carnegieeurope. eu/2015/08/13/russia-s-challenge-to-international-order-pub-61059 (accessed October 2, 2016).

Sputnik News (2015), "Lavrov Sees No 'Objective Reasons' for New Cold War", February 27, available at: https://sputniknews.com /politics/201502271018830103/ (accessed November 21, 2016).

Stavridis, J. (2016), "Avoiding the New Cold War With Russia", *Foreign Policy*, April 20, available at: http://foreignpolicy. com/2016/04/20/avoiding-the-new-cold-war-with-russia/?wp _login_ redirect=0 (accessed August 9, 2016).

The Ministry of Foreign Affairs of the Russian Federation (2013), "Concept of the Foreign Policy of the Russian Federation", February 18, available at: http://www.mid.ru/en/ foreign_policy /official_documents/-/asset_publisher/CptICkB6BZ29/content /id/122186 (accessed August 17, 2016).

The Ministry of the Foreign Affairs of the Russian Federation (2016), "Foreign Policy Concept of the Russian Federation", December 1, available at: http://www.mid.ru/en/foreign_policy / official_documents/-/asset_publisher/CptICkB6BZ29/content /id/2542248 (accessed December 10, 2016).

The White House (2010), "U.S.-Russia Relations: "Reset" Fact Sheet", June 24, available at: https://www.whitehouse.gov/the-press-office /us-russia-relations-reset-fact-sheet (accessed August 19, 2016).

Treisman, D. (2016), "Why Putin Took Crimea", *Foreign Affairs*, May/June, available at: https://www.foreignaffairs.com/articles /ukraine/2016-04-18/why-putin-took-crimea (accessed October 10, 2016).

Trenin, D. (2007), *Getting Russia Right*, Carnegie Endowment for International Peace, Washington.

Tsygankov, A. (2008a), "Russia's International Assertiveness: What Does It Mean for the West?", *Problems of Post-Communism*, Vol. 55, No. 1.

Tsygankov, A. (2008b), "Two Faces of Putin's Great Power Pragmatism", *Soviet and Post-Soviet Review*, Vol. 33, No. 1.

Wendt, A. (1992), "Anarchy is what states make of it: the social construction of power politics", *International Organization*, Vol. 46, No. 2.

Wendt, A. (1999), *Social Theory of International Politics*, Cambridge University Press, Cambridge.

Wieclawski, J. (2011), "Challenges for the Russian Foreign Policy – the Lesson of the Georgian Conflict", *Asian Social Science*, Vol. 7, No. 8.

GLOSSARY

alliances—Agreements between nations on trade, military activities, or other matters that develop strong, mutually beneficial relations.

arms race—The rapid escalation of military power, specifically nuclear weapons, that took place between the United States and the Soviet Union.

Berlin Wall—A wall built by the Soviets in 1961 that divided East and West Berlin.

capitalism—An economic system that prioritizes deregulation of markets and privatization of industry.

Cold War—A conflict between the Soviet Union and the United States that lasted from 1947 to 1991, but never included direct military action.

Communist economic policy—An economic system based on collectivism rather than the private market.

disinformation—Incorrect information presented as fact with the intention of misleading the audience.

global order—The power structure that governs world relations, including alliances and rivalries that shape trade, military action, and cultural exchange.

nuclear power—A state with nuclear weapons and the capacity to use them as a weapon.

proxy war—A conflict in which opposing sides are funded and supported by rival nations, creating an indirect conflict between them.

Security Council—Council of the United Nations, made up of five permanent member states and a rotation of other states, that votes on the most crucial issues to go before the institution.

Soviet Union—A bloc of nations, including Russia, Ukraine, Belarus, and others, that came under the leadership of Moscow through an indirect, centralized communist government.

space race—The competition between the United States and the Soviet Union to explore space, put a man on the moon, and reach other technological and scientific achievements.

spheres of influence—A form of political power in which states maintain near-sole influence over a specific region or part of the world.

treaties—Official documents between nations that govern their political relationship.

FOR MORE INFORMATION

FURTHER READING

Bodden, Valerie. *The Cold War*. New York, NY: Creative Education, 2007.

Chen, Jian. *Mao's China and the Cold War*. Chapel Hill, NC: University of North Carolina Press, 2001.

Gaddis, John Lewis. *The Cold War: A New History*. New York, NY: Penguin Books, 2006.

Hurt, Avery Elizabeth. *Superpower Rivalries and Proxy Warfare*. New York, NY: Cavendish Square, 2017.

Kallen, Stuart A. *The Cold War: Primary Sources*. New York, NY: Lucent, 2003.

Kennedy, Robert F. *Thirteen Day: A Memoir of the Cuban Missile Crisis*. New York, NY: WW Norton, 1999.

Lucas, Edward. *The New Cold War: Putin's Russia and the Threat to the West*. New York, NY: St Martin's Griffin, 2014.

Service, Robert. *The End of the Cold War: 1985–1991*. New York, NY: PublicAffairs, 2015.

Westad, Odd Arne. *The Cold War: A World History*. New York, NY: Basic Books, 2017.

Westad, Odd Arne. *The Global Cold War: Third World Interventions and the Making of Our Times*. Cambridge, UK: Cambridge University Press, 2007.

WEBSITES

Council on Foreign Relations (CFR)
www.CFR.org
This think-tank focuses on international issues and regional politics, including Russian affairs and US foreign policy. Their website features expert research, time lines, and other useful resources.

Office of the Director of National Intelligence (DNI)
www.DNI.gov
The DNI is a good resource for US intelligence information, including briefs and explainers on research being done on activities around the world.

INDEX

ABOUT THE EDITOR

Bridey Heing is a writer and book critic based in Washington, DC. She holds degrees in political science and international affairs from DePaul University and Washington University in Saint Louis. Her areas of focus are comparative politics and Iranian politics. Her master's thesis explores the evolution of populist politics and democracy in Iran since 1900. She has written about Iranian affairs, women's rights, and art and politics for publications like the *Economist*, *Hyperallergic*, and the *Establishment*. She also writes about literature and film. She enjoys traveling, reading, and exploring Washington, DC's many museums.